Coaching Psychological Skills in Youth Football: Developing The 5Cs

Chris Harwood

Richard Anderson

Published in 2015 by Bennion Kearny Limited.

Copyright © Bennion Kearny Ltd 2015

ISBN: 978-1-909125-88-9

Published by Bennion Kearny Limited
6 Woodside
Churnet View Road
Oakamoor
ST10 3AE

www.BennionKearny.com

Image Credits, pages 4, 6, muzsy/Shutterstock.com;

To my parents, Keith and Anne: I couldn't have asked for better role models in shaping the 5Cs within me – for sport and for life

Chris

Dedicated to my parents, Brian and Karen and brother Christopher.

Rich

Acknowledgements

This book would not have been possible without the ongoing professional support of many people. We would like to express our gratitude to Andy Cale who offered invaluable assistance and encouragement in the early formation of this book. We are also very grateful to the contribution made by Paul Bourne in allowing us to draw upon his vast experience and insight from going through the original 5C education programme and flying with the principles in his Academy age group coaching. Thanks must also go to Dr. Matthew Pain at the Football Association and Joe Sargison for their time and effort in using their knowledge and experience to work through the book and ensure that it is a valuable educational tool for coaches and players at all levels. Finally, special thanks must also go to the Academy staff at Nottingham Forest Football Club. They have played a hugely in important role in the original 5C intervention study and in many 5C related projects thereafter.

About the Authors

Dr Chris Harwood is a Registered Sport Psychologist and a High Performance Sport Scientist accredited by the British Association of Sport and Exercise Sciences. As a leading academic and practitioner in sport psychology at Loughborough University he has worked within applied sport psychology for the past 20 years and devotes a special interest to the Psychology of Youth Sport. He has previously served as Club Psychologist for Nottingham Forest FC, and continues to coordinate and advise on the psychology support provision for a number of professional club academy programmes. A former tennis player and coach to a national level, Chris serves on the Football Association's Psychology Advisory Board and acts as a Level 5 course tutor.

Richard Anderson, MSc, is an UEFA A-license football coach who has worked at several football clubs at youth and senior level. He is actively involved with the Football Association as a licensed tutor for their psychology development courses for coaches, as well as the production of psychology-based education resources focused on the application of psychological skills in team environments, through the work of the coach. Richard is also a former student within the School of Sport, Exercise and Health Sciences at Loughborough University. He graduated with a BSc in Sport and Exercise Science in 2007 and gained an MSc in Sport and Exercise Psychology in 2009.

Table of Contents

Foreword

Psychology has always been a key element in the development and performance of young footballers – and it is important for the grassroots player as much as it is for the academy player. As a former player now responsible for youth player development, I know that mental skills matter on and off the pitch and I have always believed that psychological skills can be nurtured and trained from a very early age.

Football clubs have the opportunity with coaches and parents to create the right environments for engaging the motivation and enthusiasm of youngsters. This is a starting point that leads to the development of other psychological strengths: the ability to remain focused, to manage mistakes and bounceback from adversity, and to maintain belief through rough patches of form. There is also the imperative of being a great team player, and developing those qualities associated with leadership and trust.

Great communicators in the dressing room and on the pitch play their role in coordinating and managing play, and giving their teammates a sense of the people that they can rely upon. It's for this reason that we adopt a focus on the 5Cs (commitment, communication, concentration, control and confidence) at our club and have done so for over 10 years. We inherently believe that we can develop the psychological strengths of our players using a simple, user-friendly framework that players, coaches and parents can readily understand.

This book brings sport psychology into the coach's home – the club training environment – and enriches the coach with relevant knowledge and practices that will help them to 'coach' and shape these critical psychological skills in their players. There is an exceptional focus on helping coaches to put mental skills on the map for young players and raise their awareness of the role of commitment, of concentration, communication skills, self-control and confidence. There is also an emphasis on challenging the coach to reflect on how he or she actually integrated mental skills into their session content. What did you actually do in today's session that might shape the psychological skills, attitudes or approach of your players? Beyond each of the chapters on each 'C', and the principles for coaching each 'C' in typical training sessions, there is an excellent case discussion by one of our former coaches who applied the 5Cs approach with his young squad.

I highly recommend this book for helping coaches to develop their own confidence in psychology, as well as to develop the mental and personal qualities of their players.

Gary Brazil. Academy Manager, Nottingham Forest FC

1

The role of psychology in football

Once again you're stood, frustrated, in the technical area as the ball nestles into the back of the net. Despairingly you gaze up to the sky before looking back to the pitch to see your opponents celebrating - their team spirit and togetherness as evident as the scoreline. Your goalkeeper and central defenders are slumped on the floor dejected, whilst a few other players solemnly trudge back to the half-way line, refusing to make eye contact with each other. A feeling of disbelief takes over; it's happened again. There's barely any time left for the re-start. Your heart sinks as the referee brings the game to an end. Once more you've allowed your opponents to get back into the game. You've switched off and conceded late on. Again it's cost you the game. All the hard work and perseverance you showed has been shattered and all that's left to give is the same debrief you feel you've been giving week after week:

"We can't keep going on like this. We can't keep giving the opposition chances to get back into the game. We can't keep falling apart when we're under pressure. You need to be tougher than that...

...Above all, how have we ended up losing a game we should have won?"

The widening role of the modern day coach

Terms like 'psychology' or 'psychologists' have tended to divide opinion within the football industry. Within the field of coaching, it is understandable that both knowledge and perceptions of the diverse nature of sport psychology will vary amongst coaches who have very similar technical and tactical expertise in the game. However, what is perhaps more constant across coaches is an acknowledgement that psychology is important and that characteristics such as mental toughness, motivation, and composure matter to development and performance. These characteristics, of course, are not only exclusive to players. Possession of these qualities is relevant for coaches, managers, support staff, and even parents given the demands of the modern game at youth and senior levels.

There are many books and resources in the football marketplace nowadays that focus on psychology. This book distinguishes itself by focusing directly on the youth coach's role and the knowledge required to become confident in implementing a system with young players that will help them to develop. The development that we are talking about here lies not only in terms of qualities related to mental toughness, but also in terms of psychological health, personal well-being, and social skills. These qualities matter for all young players to thrive in the game, regardless of the level to which their talent is ultimately nurtured.

This book is aimed at 'believers' and 'not yet believers'. If you are a 'believer' who sees the value of a psychological approach to player development and want to pick up new ideas to integrate into your coaching practice, then this book will serve your initiative. If you are a 'not yet believer' who is sceptical, fearful, and lacking in confidence around psychology, then this book will challenge your beliefs by arming you with knowledge about how you can make a developmental difference to your youth players. Along the way, it will most probably reinforce many of the coaching practices and behaviours that already represent you as a coach.

There is certainly a widening role for the coach in contemporary football and this involves your psychological inputs to player development. Alongside a specialist sport psychologist who would work to support you and your players in greater depth, you have a significant educational and behavioural role with young players on training and matchday.

Whilst mental skills aren't as easily measurable as physical performances on the Yo-Yo test, they are highly visible on the pitch through the attitudes, behaviours, and responses of players to different game situations. They are also highly measurable in 'good-bad' terms within the public sphere with clear judgements made about the mental skills and behaviour of players in off-field social situations and how players cope with lifestyle issues. Put simply, the opportunities to demonstrate psychological skills lie everywhere in football and they often arrive in quick succession.

Psychological skills are required to cope with stressful and demanding situations. How well players 'step up' in managing these challenging circumstances is partly a reflection of the quality of your coaching. When players demonstrate thoughtful, composed and mature responses, both on and off the pitch, there should be a part of you that privately feels a sense of pride in your coaching of that player. Equally, when one of your players punches an opponent, freezes under pressure, or castigates a teammate – actions which negatively influence the game and the team – then a responsible part of you should be looking at yourself and asking the 'Why?' question in search of reasonable and proactive answers.

With the aim of helping coaches to feel an increasing sense of responsibility for the psychological development of their players, this book focuses on two key developmental phases - the Foundation Phase, dealing with players aged from 8 to 11 years, and the Youth Development Phase, which includes players from 12 to 16 years of age. We feel that it is important to get the basics switched on early so that players start learning about appropriate behaviours within the Foundation Phase. This sets them up well for training and executing mental skills that are important during the Youth Development phase. Subsequently, on reaching the Professional Development Phase (16-21 years), coaches will be in receipt of a more psychologically and socially adept footballer who is in a better place to make the transitional adjustments required by a potential professional player.

Psychology in the language of football

In order to show how the psychological approach taken in this book is completely grounded within the nature and demands of football, we have created a timeline script of how the match unfolded between the two Under-16 teams introduced at the start of this chapter. We will highlight the positive and 'not-so-positive' psychological behaviours and responses that are common from players within each phase *through the language* that is often used to describe players and game events. Coaches may find it interesting to see how often basic psychological terms are used that ultimately influence players and the match as a whole.

The First Half

8 minutes into the first half: Your team has made a **fast tempo** start. They are not allowing the opposition to get any rhythm, pressing high up the pitch, tracking runners and matching them tackle-for-tackle. There's a real **eagerness to engage** in the match as quickly as possible and set the tone of the game. In contrast your opponents just haven't got going yet. There isn't the same level of **commitment** on show. Passes are tentative and the tempo slow. They can't match the **energy** that your team has started with.

18 minutes into the first half: Good **vision** from your holding midfielder has seen him play a superb pass towards your overlapping right back, in behind the opposition left back. He reaches the by-line and cuts the ball back to your striker. The goalkeeper scrambles across his goal. All the striker has to do is hit the target. Instead the striker **tenses up** and sends the ball sailing over the crossbar. A glorious opportunity to go 1-0 up has been missed. Very quickly your captain, who was also up for that attack, runs across to your striker and **encourages** him to keep getting into those positions. He tells him "you'll get the next one!"

29 minutes into the first half: The missed chance seems to have kick-started the opposition. Their left midfielder receives the ball, drops his shoulder, and beats your right back on the inside. As he goes past him, a covering midfielder clips his heels in a desperate attempt to win the ball. The left midfielder picks himself up off the floor and puts the ball down for the free kick, whilst his teammates set themselves up for the delivery.

The referee calls over your central midfielder. Your central midfielder throws his arms up in **frustration** with the referee and begins to **argue**. The referee asks him to **calm** down. Several of his teammates come across trying to persuade the referee not to show a yellow card. But it is of no use as his momentary loss of **control** leads the referee to issue him with a needless booking.

40 minutes into the first half: Your striker spins his marker on the left-hand corner of the box and is through on the goalkeeper 1v1. The opponent's central defender has been caught too tight. Two of your midfielders have burst forwards, in support, having broken free from their markers. But your striker is so **focused** on the goalkeeper and scoring himself that he isn't **aware** of the support he has. There is a simple pass across goal for a teammate to tap in, but instead the striker decides to take the ball around the goalkeeper. The goalkeeper **reads it** though and smothers the ball. The striker stands burying his head in his hands. Your midfielders stand and **criticise** him for not squaring the ball across goal for a simple tap in.

After claiming the ball, the opposition goalkeeper **refocuses** and has sprung a quick counter attack, kicking the ball long upfield. Your team are **out of position**. You've overcommitted during the last attack and players haven't **tracked back**. It's two-against-two in defence. One of their midfielders **drives** forwards making it three-against-two. Your midfielders **give up** tracking back. They are resigned to what is about to happen. Their striker **gets his head up** and sees his midfielder's forward run, playing a perfectly weighted through-ball to him. Unlike your striker at the opposite end, he keeps his **composure** and rounds the goalkeeper to score. It's against the run of play but you find yourselves 0-1 behind with five minutes left to play in the first half.

1 minute into stoppage time: The goal has given the opposition an added **drive**, whilst your team **look** shell-shocked. The goal most definitely has knocked you out of your stride. The team's **cohesion** and **discipline** has suffered. The opponents pass the ball from teammate to teammate, as your central midfielders chase the ball, desperately trying to win it back. A poor first touch leaves one of your central midfielders thinking he has an opportunity to pinch the ball. He dives into the tackle but mistimes it, sending the player crashing to the floor. The opposition players surround the referee. Your central midfielder has already been booked. They demand he be sent-off. The referee is left with no choice other than to produce a second yellow card and send him off. It's a cruel way to finish the half but your team goes in 0-1 down and now also a player down.

The Second Half

13 minutes into the second half: Your players have re-grouped at the start of the second half. You've re-organised during half-time and are showing a **persistence** not to allow the opposition to dictate the game. Your captain is leading from the front, giving out instructions, demanding lots of **effort** from your team. The players are responding. It leaves you with hope that you may overcome the adverse circumstances and find a way back into the game. But the goal and sending off at the end of the first half have given the opposition **confidence**. They have come out with a **positive attitude** and more **determination** than they had at the start of the first half.

20 minutes into the second half: Your right winger receives the ball, played into him from the right back. He is encouraged to be **positive** and beat the full back on his own. Dropping a shoulder he crosses the ball into the box but the opposition central defender wins the header comfortably and clears it out of the box. The header, however, only falls as far as your central midfielder who controls the ball and decides to take an optimistic strike at goal from 30 yards.

As the ball sails towards the goal, it takes a deflection off of an opposition player, leaving the goalkeeper wrong-footed and rolls into the net. A fortuitous goal to score but it has your team back in the game and gives them something to fight for in the last 25 minutes.

In response the opposition players look around at each other supporting and encouraging one another. They urge each other to remain **composed** and focus their attention on getting the ball back quickly. 1-1.

33 minutes into the second half: Since the equaliser your team have been put under pressure by the opposition. Your players are becoming more and more **anxious** in possession. Each time a pass goes astray another player begins to **hide**. Nobody wants to let the side down but at the same time they are **fearful** of being the one to give the ball away. Passes are being sent long and the ball just keeps coming back as your team desperately try to hold on to what they have.

This has given your opponents a growing **belief** that they can get a second goal in the time remaining. They have been more successful in raising their **intensity** since conceding. Dominating the ball has seen them create chance after chance, but they have been unsuccessful in finding the important break-through as you enter the final 15 minutes of the game.

2 minutes into stoppage time at the end of the game: Your team is still **working hard** but their **body language** is that of a tired team who don't look **confident** they can hold out as fatigue takes its toll.

The opposition's attacks have been relentless in the previous 15 minutes, as yet another attack forces a corner and one final opportunity to win the game. As the ball is delivered in, your goalkeeper misjudges the flight of the ball and it sails over him onto the head of the opposition central defender. Fortunately your right back on the post has moved to cover the goalkeeper and divert the header off the line and over the bar for another corner. Your goalkeeper and right back exchange words, as the right back **criticises** the goalkeeper and demands that he "**switches on**" for the next corner.

The second corner is delivered close to the goal. Your central defender calls on your goalkeeper to come and claim the cross, but the goalkeeper, **worried** about misjudging the ball again, stays on his line. An opposition striker takes advantage of this by attacking the ball unopposed to bullet a header into the back of the net from four yards out. There is barely any time left for the restart, as the referee brings the game to an end. 1-2.

Full Time

From the first to the last minute, the game poses challenges that will test players' psychological skills. How well a player has developed, understands, and is in control of their behaviours and responses to these challenges, will help determine how well they can impose themselves on the game. Re-reading the match narrative and taking note of the highlighted words and phrases, you may have noticed that there are an abundance of behaviours that are important to performance from a psychological perspective. Given that all of these behaviours have a potential impact on match performance, it is important for the coach to be aware of them and their implications. Below are just a selection of the behaviours the players from both teams demonstrated during the match described over the previous pages.

Fig 1.1: A selection of individual positive and negative psychological behaviours and responses that can be seen during a football match to the benefit or detriment of a team

Looking back to the future

The colour codes for these words, above, will become apparent soon. However, let's pause for a moment and rewind the clock. As each player's journey to match day begins on the training pitch, let's take a look - back in time - at what could have been happening with these players years earlier when they were being coached in weekly training session. We've seen the types of behaviour which occur during the game - so what behaviours may have been operating on the training pitch in the way these players were coached? We will examine the training sessions of two hypothetical squads - an Under-10 and Under-11 group within the Foundation Phase.

As the coaches take their teams through a warm-up, into the main session, and conclude with a cool down, please consider what behaviours represent the engagement of these players to the session and its tasks? More importantly, consider the impact that the coach is having on these behaviours during the session, and *why* they are having such an impact?

Start of training: The warm up

The coaches of the under 10 team arrive early and have already set up for the session. As each player arrives, one of the coaches tells the players to get a ball and join him in a small grid he has set up to the side of the training area. The coach asks the players to show him how many different parts of their feet they can use to turn, dribble, and run with the ball, as they move around the grid. The coach walks around the grid encouraging those who are attempting new skills. The exercise acts as a bridge between the players' arrival and the session starting, keeping those who have turned up early engaged in a task as they wait for everyone to arrive. Not long after the last player turns up, the coach calls an end to the exercise. As the coach talks, each player listens attentively, making eye contact with the coach, facing him, as he informs them of what is going to happen next.

The players move next into their warm up. There is a **spring in the players' steps** with lots of visible **effort** and **enjoyment**. The coach praises players for their effort and encourages them to also praise each other when they see someone on their team do something well. The coach is quick to reinforce those players who have supported each other.

The Under-11 coaches arrive late to the session so the players have been standing around waiting. Once the coaches turn up, the players start **preparing** for the session - rummaging through the bag of balls to find ones that aren't flat. They then proceed to take shots at goal as they wait until the session begins. Once it appears that no more players are turning up for the session, the coaches call in the players. They stand talking to the players at length about their previous game telling them who played well and who didn't, before talking about what they need to do in their next game. Some players try to listen but lose interest, whilst others are distracted by the training session from the Under-10's team which is taking place on the adjacent pitch.

The players are then sent for a warm up jog around the perimeter of the pitch several times. During this time the two coaches discuss what they should do during the training session. As the players jog around the pitch, some of the players stay at the back so they can have a laugh and joke and generally be disruptive to those players at the front who want to warm-up for the session the best they can.

The main session

Immediately after the warm up the Under-10's coaches quickly **engage** the players in what the learning outcomes for the session are going to be. Prior to each practice the coaches remind the players of what they are trying to achieve and set up **aims** for the forthcoming practice.

Each player is actively involved at all times with lots of variety. The practices build on the previous one, **progressively becoming more challenging** for the players. The players themselves look **relaxed** and **confident**, with everyone wanting the ball and **not being afraid** to take on the challenges that the coaches pose them. When mistakes are made the players just carry on and continue to **try hard** in a very **energetic** manner throughout the session.

The coaches themselves make sure to go around all the groups and **encourage** the players individually for their **effort** or for the good work they show on the ball. When something breaks down a coach is on hand to help give personal **feedback** whilst still **reinforcing** the good work they have been doing. All players, whether they are succeeding or struggling with the task, receive the same attention from the coach.

For the final 15 minutes of the session the coaches organise the players into a match. They challenge the players to demonstrate what they have learnt during the session and to not be afraid; to **keep trying** even if they don't find success immediately. Whenever a player performs an improved skill from the session, coaches are vigilant in spotting this and acknowledging the player.

In contrast the Under-11 team have very little variety to their training session. Players are standing around waiting for their turn at the drill and are having very few touches on the ball. Slowly they begin to lose interest, become **bored**, and start to mess about. As a result the coaches grow more **annoyed** with the players as the session goes on.

Some of the exercises are proving too difficult for the players. Only the best players in the team are coping and the practices keep breaking down. The better players lay the **blame** for this at those players who are struggling. One player begins to **sulk** at being on the receiving end of some of his teammates' **criticism**. The coaches begin dealing with this by stopping the practice and publicly telling the players that what they are doing is wrong and what they should be doing better. As some players continue to struggle, the coach compares them to the better players in the team. "Watch what Tom does. That's what you need to do." Even on the occasions when they do manage some success there is a lack of **praise** and **reinforcement** from the coach. Some of the players start to **give up** or **not get involved** in order to avoid getting shouted at again.

With the late start and a lot of time spent by the coaches correcting 'mistakes' in the drills, there is only 6-7 minutes at the end of the session for a match. The better players have **stopped trying hard** by this point and are very **lethargic**. The players who have struggled throughout the session **hide away** not **wanting the ball**. The quality of the match is therefore poor, much to the **frustration** of the coaches.

Cool down

The Under-10 coaches conclude their match and call all the players in to perform a cool down. Once completed both coaches begin by **praising** the **efforts** of the players during the session. They ask the players what they **feel** they have done well during the session, what they have **learnt** and what they think they can **improve** on during the next session. Each player is given an equal opportunity to participate and add their views. It is a very interactive and player-led discussion to conclude the session.

It is a completely different ending to the session for the Under-11 team. One of the coaches calls their match to an end and gathers the players in. A few of the players ask each other "Is that it?" before asking the coach whether they can play longer. The coach tells them that they can't as they have run out of time in the session, but if the players wanted more game time they should turn up to training earlier next week. That way "we can get started sooner and get through what we need to in good time."

Once all the players are in, the coaches ask them to go and pick up all the cones and retrieve all the footballs they've used, before organising them and packing them up. Once done they are then free to go. The coaches then pick up all the equipment and leave.

End of training.

The psychological influence of the coach

Reflecting back on the training sessions from the Under-10 and Under-11 age groups, coaches may be able to contrast the psychological and social qualities that are apparent in one group compared to the lack of opportunity to experience these qualities in the other group. In fact, the only opportunity the U-11group gains is arguably the experience and shaping of more negative and dysfunctional qualities.

Reflect on how the qualities of your coaching environment impacts upon the behaviour of your player.

By looking at the influence that the coaches have on the players' experiences of training and how the interaction between the players affects that experience, coaches may be able to understand how these psychological responses translate into positive and negative actions within matches. Certainly having a clear psychological approach across coaches when working with players will help to shape the positive types of response that you want to cultivate in players across their years of development.

A coach's approach to youth players will impact on the player. Their approach will affect: the way children perceive their learning environment and if it is player-centred or not (e.g., *Am I here to learn new skills?* versus *Am I here to show how much better I am compared to everyone else?*); their attitude to new challenges ("*I will try this new skill. I may not get it first time, but I'll keep going until I get it*" versus "*This skill is too hard. Others have got it straight away. I'll do an easier skill so I get it right and look good,*"); and their perceptions of how good they feel they are. This in turn affects how motivated the players are, how well they interact with teammates, and their ability to focus and deal with setbacks.

For completeness, a summary of the behaviours that were demonstrated during both training sessions is presented below. Notice the similar colour coding.

Fig 1.2a: Positive psychological behaviours and responses shown by the players and the coach during the under 10 training session

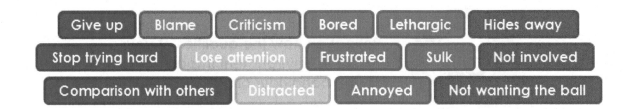

*Fig 1.2b: Negative psychological behaviours and responses shown
by the players and the coach during the under 11 training session*

Introducing the '5Cs'

It should already be clear that there are a wide variety of behaviours and responses on show during training and matches, and not all of them are desirable. One of the main aims of this book is to help you as the coach identify these behaviours and recognise their potential impact upon performance. Then, through conscious effort and a targeted approach, you will be in a better position to have a more positive and consistent impact on your player's psychological skills.

Take a moment to look back again at the colour coded list of behaviours shown by the player during training and matches. Invariably, these behaviours and responses bear close similarities to each other and can be grouped based upon their relation to a player's level of **commitment**, their **communication** skills, their ability to **concentrate**, their self-**control**, and their overall **confidence**, as shown below.

Fig 1.3: Player behaviour and responses shown in training and/or match play can be grouped together based on their relation to commitment, communication, concentration, control or confidence

Collectively these are known as the 5Cs and represent what we consider to be the important components of positive psycho-social development in players. When one considers a player who is thriving in the game, then this is most probably a player who is highly motivated, able to regulate their emotions and their attention appropriately, and a player who has good interpersonal skills. These characteristics may indeed underpin mentally tough and emotionally intelligent players who both challenge themselves whilst maintaining effective relationships with others.

We believe that the 5Cs should form the spine of psychological and social skill development for every competitive youth soccer player. Therefore, the aim of the 5Cs program in this book is to increase the awareness and confidence of coaches with respect to their ability to coach these psycho-social skills so that young players benefit from their development.

At the core of the 5Cs is a player's commitment. This motivational quality drives the player within their training and matches. It is characterised by players who show consistent effort, high quality preparation, and a desire for learning; players who focus on making improvements and progressing from their mistakes. Having high levels of commitment holds the 5Cs together, because without the appropriate quality of motivation, the other Cs will not function effectively.

Building on the foundation of commitment is communication. Communication represents a player's ability to relate to others (e.g., teammates, coaches, parents) through how they send and receive information to and from each other. It is an interpersonal quality that is characterised by players who share information, ask helpful questions, listen respectfully, and accept feedback. Players with good communication skills strive to be highly coachable as well as being able to communicate non-verbally, alongside encouraging and instructing their teammates clearly and confidently.

The next critical C is concentration. This is essentially a player's ability to focus on the right thing, at the right time. It is characterised by players who focus on a task through to a conclusion and stay focused on key components of a task in the midst of many potential distractions that compete for the player's attention. Concentration is strongly linked to a player's control skills which also rely heavily on the quality of a player's commitment and communication abilities.

Control is characterised by a player's ability to regulate their thoughts, feelings and emotions in order to manage their behaviour and performance. Players with expert control know how to apply, direct, and ration their available mental and emotional energy in response to a specific situation, event, or task on and off the pitch. Such players remain composed yet alert, implement breathing and other relaxation techniques, and display positive, helpful reactions to themselves and others following mistakes, poor officiating decisions and other game events.

The final C, confidence, is the outcome of well-developed commitment, communication, concentration and control. It is the belief that a player has in executing a skill to a desired level or achieving a specific outcome. It is characterised by players who try new skills, take calculated risks, show strong body language, and stay involved in the game. Such players consistently 'play brave' and want the ball regardless of the scoreline or time left in the match.

The model below outlines these interactions between each of the Cs, and acts as a starting point in aiding your understanding of the 5Cs.

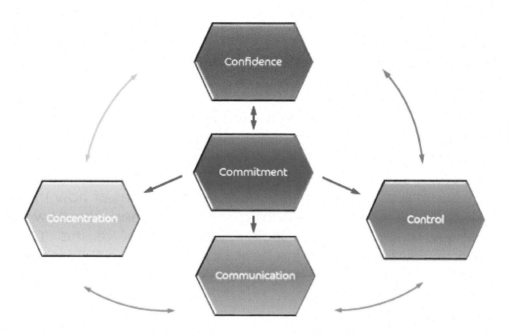

Fig 1.4: The interactions of the 5Cs

The 5Cs are psychological and social qualities that help young athletes to 'play brave' in training and competition.

The purpose and structure of this book

Football coaches pride themselves on their technical and tactical knowledge, and applying this knowledge to help young players is a tremendously motivating and rewarding experience. Likewise, influencing and shaping a player's psychological and social qualities is a significant and valuable undertaking for a coach. It is a mission in which coaches play a vital developmental role. Therefore, the 5Cs program is designed to weave these psychological skills into the fabric of your normal technical and tactical coaching practice, at developmental stages when your players are most open to psychological skills training.

This book follows a similar structure to the first 5C education-intervention project that was conducted with coaches in a professional football academy. We will focus on introducing each 'C' one by one, as we go through chapters on:

Chapter 1

- Raising Awareness
- Enhancing Knowledge
- Proposing Applications and Practices

A chapter will be devoted to each 'C' within which we first introduce the 'C' and outline specific behaviours associated with it. We then educate coaches further with what we feel is fundamental knowledge for the coach to possess, before presenting strategies and practices that can be integrated into typical coaching session plans. We subsequently offer examples of how the 'C' can be integrated into the yearly coaching curriculum, and also how coaches can self-review and reflect on their implementation of the 'C' in their coaching practice. The heart of the book covers all of the 5C's sequentially in this manner.

- Chapter 3 – Commitment
- Chapter 4 – Communication
- Chapter 5 – Concentration
- Chapter 6 – Control
- Chapter 7 – Confidence

Beyond focusing on the actual 5C's themselves, we have also developed a set of principles that coaches can follow when integrating each 'C' into their coaching. Derived from education, research and personal experience, we believe these are useful guidelines in helping players to understand the 5C's and to normalise mental skills as something that are totally fundamental to their development; not something that should be viewed with fear or scepticism. The next chapter (Chapter 2) discusses these principles under the acronym 'PROGRESS' so that coaches are ready for the subsequent chapters where each 'C' is introduced. You will notice some of the principles coming through in the practices of each 'C', and we therefore recommend that you read this chapter first before reading about each 'C' in depth.

Finally, we will complete the book with an example case study from a coach who has gone through the 5C journey upon which you are now embarking. This real-life discussion focuses on how this coach used his increased awareness and knowledge around the key principles, skills and behaviours of the 5Cs and incorporated them into his normal coaching routine. We hope that the true-to-life coaching episodes presented in this section will consolidate the principles covered within the book. Moreover, we hope that it serves as an ongoing resource to refer back to in order to help you reflect on your own experiences in weaving each 'C' into your training programme.

Whilst our advice for youth coaches is to work through each 'C' one by one and practice through trial and error, we do encourage you to read the whole book first. In this way, you will gain a clearer feel and understanding for the whole system and the holistic strength of the 5C's as a total, integrated approach. From this foundation of knowledge, you can decide how you want to go about making advancements and changes in your coaching. We do encourage inexperienced coaches to focus on each single 'C' for a few weeks (e.g. 4-6 sessions) before moving on because it will lead to the development of a stronger repertoire of experience and practice for the following season when coaches can start integrating and reinforcing multiple 'C's at once in a given session.

Most importantly, we hope that the book builds your confidence as a coach, and that you feel the benefits from a growing, practical knowledge of sport psychology in youth soccer.

2

Making PROGRESS with the 5Cs

In this chapter, we introduce the eight key principles and processes that lie at the heart of the coach's methodology in shaping mental skills in their players. These principles are not complicated and many would argue that they represent merely educational 'common sense'. We agree. However, common sense is not always commonly practiced and it is easy to forget certain principles of effective coaching and learning. Our aim here is to remind coaches of the key ways in which a mental skill can be (a) understood; (b) valued; (c) practiced; (d) trained under pressure; (e) supported; and (f) reviewed by players. In this respect, coaches have the best chance of supporting their players to integrate and learn the psychological and social skills that will help them to manage the demands of football and enjoy the game.

Each of the eight principles will be presented with practical examples of how they can be applied when working with each of the subsequent 'Cs' in the chapters that follow.

Principle 1: Promote the 'C'

Technical, tactical and physical skills are viewed as important by young players because coaches talk about them all the time. They promote them intentionally because they are valued. If coaches want players to value mental skills then coaches should **intentionally promote** the chosen 'C' in the same way as they introduce a technical or tactical skill. Mental skills represent important performance factors, and if the coach does not give equal attention and 'playing time' to mental skills, then players will not internalise the importance and relevance of the mental skill fully.

Regardless of the age group of your players, you can draw players' attention to each of the 'Cs', and show them how much you value the development of that 'C' as a coach. For each of the 'Cs', you have the opportunity to engage young players in what the meaning of the 'C' actually is.

Coaches need to give 'playing time' to mental skills if they want them to develop in players.

For example, whether it is before training, at the start of, or during the session, offer players the opportunity to draw out and tell you what they see in:

- a committed, motivated player vs a non-committed player
- an excellent communicator vs a poor communicator
- a highly focused player vs a player with poor concentration
- a calm and composed player vs a player with no self-control
- a highly confident player vs a player with low confidence

There are several core behaviours for each 'C' listed in each separate chapter, and this is a key awareness-promoting strategy that coaches can adapt for most ages. It is important that coaches devote time to this principle and keep returning to it with players, picking out key behaviours associated with each 'C'. Many young players will be experiencing new thoughts and feelings for the first time in their lives, and wanting to attach meaning to them. For example, most players will know what it feels like to be angry and very nervous, but they need help in identifying why these emotions occur and how they can manage them. Many young players may not understand some of the emotions that they are feeling for the first time, and some may tend to think that they are the **only ones** feeling this way. To realise that emotions are normal, experienced by all players, and that they are not alone can be a great relief to the young player. Your role is therefore to normalise that emotions happen, and help players to share and discuss the types of feelings that they can have, and how they can learn to master their feelings.

This awareness will enhance their value in practicing different training techniques associated with Control (our 4th 'C') from a young age. However, this principle applies to all of the 'Cs'. Therefore, promote the 'C' and help players to understand what it means from an early age.

Principle 2: Role model the 'C'

As a follow-on from promoting the 'C', ensure that you use the power of role models and visual demonstrations for young players. One of the key methods for helping players to understand the 'C' is for you, yourself, to role model the 'best' and the 'worst' examples of behaviour associated with that 'C'. For example, what would a footballer with the 'worst concentration ever' look like? Have fun with players drawing out the differences, and why not challenge them to have a go at demonstrating the best vs worst qualities? You'll see a number of exercises in the forthcoming chapters that task players to have fun 'acting as if' they are 'the best and the worst players ever' at that mental skill.

Beyond using yourself as a model, or other players, you can use video footage of (elite) players, and also ask players to think of which professional players they think are the best role models associated with that 'C'. Which role models are the best communicators, and why? Which players do they think are consistently the most confident, and why?

The use of other sports is also encouraged as players begin to appreciate what the **positive outcomes and consequences** are for players possessing high levels of each 'C', compared to the **problems and limitations** of being poor at that specific 'C'.

Consistent modelling and demonstrations of each 'C' can form a complementary part of any practice, drill, and certainly open game situation. Of course, it also goes without saying that the coach can role model the 5C's in all of their interactions with players, coaching staff, and parents. Role modelling therefore extends to 'who coaches are' and how they live their 5C values, as well as 'what they coach'.

Principle 3: Ownership of their learning

Giving players a sense of ownership is an important motivational strategy for coaches as you will see in Chapter 3 on Commitment. Players are more motivated to learn, perform, and persist at new skills when they are the origin of the decision to engage in the task or skill. Coaches can offer players a greater sense of ownership by involving them in decisions within sessions and helping them to see a clear rationale (helped by Principle 2).

Firstly, navigate your promotion and discussion of each 'C' to points where the players are the ones coming up with the agreed values and behaviours to work on in each session, or a specific practice. The younger players will need some assistance here as a collective, but the aim is to involve players in agreeing what the core values and behaviours are that everyone signs up to trying, supporting and reinforcing in the session, exercise or practice. For example:

- How do we want to show that we are all committed players?
- What effective ways of communicating to each other are we going to sign up to today?
- How are we going to be the most focused squad possible in this week's sessions?
- What ways can we all practice being the coolest and most composed players on the pitch this week?
- What behaviours represent our 'squad rules' to keep our confidence levels high during this training session?

Secondly, where possible, offer players options to spend more time on a skill at their individual level. There may be several opportunities to orchestrate choices in your sessions whereby players have the option of concentrating on one drill or skill or moving onto another option. In this respect, you are helping them to calibrate themselves for what will be an optimal challenge for them. Ensure that one option is not more valued or correct than another, and that you set the tone that persisting at improving one skill is just as important as trying a new skill. It is the player's choice and responsibility to select what they want to learn. Thirdly, in taking a strengths-based approach to your coaching, ensure that you offer players the option of doing one of their favourite/feel good drills or practices. This is a principle discussed under the Confidence 'C' that helps players to build positive memories and a sense of accomplishment from the session.

Principle 4: Grow the 'C'

This fourth principle relates to the opportunities that coaches give to help players practice each 'C' and teach to their individual needs. For instance, communication skills are more likely to develop when conditions are set around using instructions, listening, encouragement and praise. For example, only allowing one player to talk per team will allow the player to practice their verbal **communication** skills and the coach to assess this player's current communication strengths. It will also allow the rest of the squad to practice their non-verbal communication skills and recognise the importance of these. Likewise, self-**control** is more likely to develop when players are tasked with shouting positive self-talk immediately after a mistake or error in order to train their ability to 'bounce back' immediately (and publically too!). In each 'C' chapter the coach will be introduced to drills that allow players to practice and 'train' their 'Cs' over time. In open game situations, alongside other conditions and distractions (e.g., one player down, poor refereeing, time pressure), the team and individuals' performance of the 5C's can be challenged and tested under greater stress.

Principle 5: Reinforce the 'C'

As with any technical skill, positive reinforcement from the coach when a player demonstrates an appropriate psychological response will help to develop the player's competence and confidence in that mental skill. Therefore, within the 5C philosophy, coaches are encouraged to privately and also publically praise players as they make efforts to demonstrate behaviours associated with each 'C'.

One of the key tasks for coaches is to be attentive to teachable moments when they see a direct link between the (extra) efforts of players and a directly positive outcome (e.g., a goal, free kick, goal saving tackle, quick regain/re-possession). It can also be related to when a coach has set an agreed performance goal or target for a drill, and players attain the goal with clear evidence of effortful behaviours. When these teachable moments occur, it is important for the coach to emphasise the value of how such commitment led to direct positives.

Through reading the Commitment chapter, your positive reinforcement of a player's persistence and effort will have a strong influence on their motivation. A coach can strengthen a player's perception of their own competence by helping them to own their improvement. Personalising the reinforcing statement offers more ownership and autonomy to a player. For example, when you say: "Matt, your dedication has brought that skill on in leaps and bounds, you have set yourself some great standards and stuck at doing the right things" - this statement is all about the player, and what they have done that they can continue to do. Contrast this with a statement such as: "That's what I want to see, you've taken my advice on board." This latter affirmation is more about you, the coach, rather than the player, and it subtly takes the ownership and personal endeavour away from the player compared with the former statement.

In addition, one of the most vital principles of reinforcement is to acknowledge and praise the decision and intention first as opposed to the quality of execution. This is discussed further in our Confidence chapter. Coaches want to **empower courage** in their players, not simply in trying out new mental skills and strategies, but also with any other technical, tactical or physical skill. To encourage players to take on new and difficult skills, the coach needs to create a 'no fear of failure' climate where players can safely persist in bravely improving themselves. Behaving as a 5C coach, players will be able to see that you understand and believe in 'learning errors' that are met with your positive and helpful support when they are naturally made by players.

23

In order to develop players with less fear, both the coach and teammates need to be attentive to praising **the courageous decision.** In this respect, regardless of the quality of execution, you target the **perception and the decision making skill** of the player. If the coach and other squad members support the decision, then the player will feel confident to persist in their learning even in the face of an execution error. When a young player repeatedly receives criticism or negative squad responses for trying something difficult but failing, then they will perceive greater **value** in not trying that skill. You will have **negatively empowered** them to protect their current ability, play safe, and avoid the possibility of any further mistakes, even when their perception and decision making may have actually been correct. Therein lies the 'fear of failure' climate that will move players backwards and precipitate 'avoidance' behaviours – the psychological toxin that is lethal to player development.

Principle 6: Empower peer support

Linked in with your reinforcement and support of the player is the central principle of peer or teammate support. What football peers think about them as a player matters a great deal to the adolescent boy or girl as they strive to fit in and measure up to their peer group. From late childhood and throughout the teenage years, children strive to develop their own identity, independence, and sense of being good at things. Adolescence is a long and arduous journey of discovering that 'I'm really OK - I've got something to offer - I can get on with others, and I can survive on my own'. Throughout this journey, they'll automatically be making comparisons with other children in the same situation as them. Because of their similarities in age, and often background, other children offer the player the standards of behaviour and ability against which they can judge themselves. The perceptions and opinions of other players, particularly those that a player respects, can be highly influential to that player. They can influence beliefs, thoughts, emotions and subsequently the decisions and actions of a player. The way that peers or teammates behave towards each other can often make or break the soccer experience for a young player.

As a coach, you serve as a guardian of the climate or learning environment that is created for players. This means, however, that you have to get a strong grip on peer influence because the behaviour of peers will possibly have a stronger impact on the adolescent player than your own values, behaviour and words of wisdom as a coach. The tone for interactions between peers, and what is praiseworthy (versus unacceptable peer behaviour) should be firmly set from the start and never deviated from.

Create a coaching climate where teammate support and praise for effort is highly valued.

In terms of the 5C's, as with technical skills, the simplest coaching standard is to **intentionally** encourage players to praise each other for their efforts, and also to make the link between effort and positive outcomes (as discussed above). For example, a peer's reinforcement of good communication to another player, or praise for attempting the right move (or pass even if it did not come off) are both powerful behaviours that will positively affect the receiver's communication, commitment, and confidence levels. When players follow through on a team 'rule' of praising dogged persistence, positive reactions after errors, or laser-beam concentration, then it is amazing to see the level of collective spirit and confidence that can develop.

Principle 7: Support the supporter

A coach closes the loop of a positive learning environment when he demonstrates the value of 'praising the praiser'. Whether or not the coach has set up a buddying practice or asked young players to wear an imaginary 5C radar or antenna that picks up when other players show a 'C', the coach creates the opportunity to acknowledge a player who offers support and praise to a teammate. This strategy shows that you care about the nature of support that players give and receive, and is a potent means of establishing not only trusting relationships with your players, but also a safe environment where players may play more freely and expressively.

Principle 8: Self-review and responsiveness

When coaches set the scene for a training session, introduce new knowledge and draw out the purpose of drills and practices, it is useful to check-in with players and monitor how they feel they are doing at specific skills. With all of the 5C's, a coach can take a quick time out to ask players what they feel their levels of effort, focus, communication, composure, and confidence are right now. Dependent on age, players could use a scale from 1-10 or, as described in subsequent chapters, they could rate and review themselves in terms of football teams in the league. This can be a fun task with a serious message behind it. It may be interesting to ask players 'what would a one league position improvement look like?' in terms of mental skills or behaviour. Having renewed the awareness that the 'C' is important, the coach can challenge players to maintain that high level or see if they can push commitment or concentration that little bit higher. Challenging this responsiveness towards the end of a session when players are tiring can pay dividends in seeing players renewing and raising their efforts right to the end.

For younger players, a coach might delegate the role of a monitor (e.g., a commitment or communication monitor) who switches on their commitment or communication radar during a practice and then gives feedback to the coach and the rest of his teammates on how they feel their squad are doing. This can be specifically introduced at a break in play, or before a transition in practice, and not only gives the opportunity of leadership to a young player, but also automatically strengthens the value of the 'C' within the peer group. Other players can be asked for their opinion on how to raise or maintain the level, and monitors can be swapped from session to session so that every team member has a go at being the 5C mental toughness monitor.

 **Take time to encourage positive self-reflection and review skills in players and the team.**

At the end of a session, we've noted how some coaches let players go and switch off without adopting a consistent routine of debriefing and reinforcing some of the key learning points or achievements in the session. To stretch young players' attention spans and help their self-reflection skills to develop, the last three minutes of a session could allow players to come up with three or four points that they learned about in the session, what they felt went well and what they feel they could improve upon next session. These golden few minutes will promote the value that you give to reviewing performance and training in a way that doesn't simply rest on outcomes or results. Consequently, players will become motivated to review themselves and their learning in terms of multiple dimensions, processes and achievements. Therefore, for the sake of just a few minutes, do not miss the opportunity to help players 'deposit' their learning and achievements (individually and collectively) in a way that will maintain their confidence and motivation.

Summarising PROGRESS

By working through these eight principles, you may have noticed that we have made **PROGRESS**! This is summarised in the table below.

Promote the 'C' in the same way that you would introduce and value a technical or tactical skill. Draw out what it means and how important it is to football.

Role-Model the 'C', bringing its meaning to life by demonstrating or referring to excellent examples, versus bad examples from football, or other sports.

Ownership of their learning. Involve players in decisions within the session about how they can demonstrate a 'C'; allow them options to work at their own pace and to benefit from favourite drills and practice that showcase their strengths.

Grow the 'C' by providing players with opportunities to practice the 'C', and then to train it in more open game situations when 'pressure' can be added to test players.

Reinforce the 'C' by praising those players who respond by demonstrating the chosen 'C' skill or behaviour, and by making courageous decisions.

Empower peer support by encouraging players to praise each other for positive efforts related to each 'C' in order to build individual and collective confidence.

Support the supporter by acknowledging those players when they achieve the above, thereby closing the loop on a supportive environment around each of the 'Cs'.

Self-review and responsiveness. Check-in with players on their levels of the 'C' and empower them to keep working hard; use monitors to review collective efforts, and apply the 'golden minutes' of 'reviewing your learning' at the end of the session.

We hope that coaches find PROGRESS to be a useful acronym to help remember the steps, behaviours, and ideas that can help to introduce, teach, develop, support, train, and review each 'C' in their players. The following chapters will now discuss each 'C' in depth so that you gain the underpinning knowledge that will empower you to integrate specific coaching behaviours and practices in your sessions.

3
Commitment

As far as psychological attributes are concerned, commitment is the central characteristic of the 5C's framework. It underpins the development and performance of the other 'Cs', and also empowers the technical and physical corners of player development. At its core, commitment represents the **quantity** and **quality** of motivation that cognitively and emotionally **drives** the young player within their football training and matches.

As a coach what you might aspire to see in the complete youth player is their ability to focus consistently on personal (and team) performance goals. You will want them to learn and problem-solve their way to success by regulating their actions and behaviours. Experiencing enjoyment and fun in the process may also be something you wish to see.

As you begin to consider what you might put on your commitment 'wish list' you may find it useful at this point to consider specifically what types of behaviours (tied to the age group you primarily work with) that you would expect and desire to see in a committed player. Whilst this is a useful task for you as a coach, working through this task with your players will draw their attention to the importance you place on developing and showing committed behaviours at all times.

An interesting switch up on this exercise is to refer back to your list of excellent commitment behaviours for your age group, but now consider what the opposite list might look like. What does a player who only focuses on outcomes, doesn't value personal improvement, and lacks commitment look like? Your own age group may contain players who are positioned at different points of the continuum from excellent-to-poor for that stage of development.

Commitment: The core behaviours

Drawing practically from long standing theories of motivation in psychology, a number of key behaviours would visibly stand out to coaches and players in training and match situations.

1. **Mental and physical effort levels** would not only be high in sessions and matches, but there would be a **consistency** to this intensity of effort across time. Levels of trying hard would be mostly unconditional.
2. **Player Engagement** in tasks, drills, games, and challenges would be something visible to the coach. These players are in the game for intrinsic reasons, love being part of the action, and this enthusiasm for involvement is very tangible, often infectious, on the pitch.
3. Players will **approach** (as opposed to **avoid**) new challenges and difficult tasks that stretch their current skill levels. They will actively look to improve themselves, and won't shy away from embracing the development of a new skill.
4. When learning a new skill, these players would demonstrate **consistent persistence** in the face of mistakes and errors. The committed player will process **learning errors;** errors or mistakes that, whilst perhaps mildly irritating at the time, offer valuable information about how to further refine and master the skill.

With respect to indicators of optimal motivation, these four components of behaviour are central to commitment regardless of age. They relate to the 8 year old as much as the 88 year old player. However, you and your coaching colleagues or team may have identified and exchanged a longer list of 'commitment' behaviours that might be more specific to your age group. Many of these behaviours will be natural 'spin offs' nourished by optimally motivated players. For example, a professional adult player who shows **excellent commitment** to their job and the team can be differentiated from the poorly committed player on a number of characteristic behaviours.

Effort, engagement, self-challenge and persistence are core attributes of the committed player.

Consider the tables below and how the 'excellent' list aligns with the four core commitment behaviours that represent the player.

A player with excellent commitment will...

- Be punctual at all times
- Strictly follow sleep, diet and hydration routines
- Conduct disciplined and structured mental and physical warm-ups for home and away matches
- Be eager to engage in the match as early as possible, when both home and away
- Track back at all times when required
- Get back into position to fulfil their role
- Make an effort to win second balls and be in the right position
- Make an effort to tackle solidly
- Make an effort to win the ball back having lost it
- Close players down and deny the opposition space, time and passing options
- Make runs even when rarely passed to
- Support play and make runs on a consistent basis and look to contribute to sustained pressure
- Make teammates' bad passes look good by chasing them down
- Renew effort and intensity after a goal has been scored whether it is for or against
- Stay involved in play and/or look to create opportunities when momentum is against the team
- Show themselves for teammates, especially when they are finding it difficult to escape the attentions of opponents
- Play through pain and/or physical fatigue

Fig 3.1.1: Characteristics of players with excellent levels of commitment

A player with poor commitment will...

- Have no clear pattern to pre-match preparation
- Only prepare mentally for home games and provide excuses when it's an away match
- Coast through warm-ups and therefore risk injury
- Sulk because they are a substitute, and won't prepare themselves optimally for the moment when they'll be needed
- Track back poorly throughout the game
- Fail to get up the field or take too long
- Fail to get back into position
- Fail to respond well to teammates' instructions or positive criticism by not taking personal responsibility
- Fail to renew effort after a goal is scored, thinking "I've done my bit!"
- Give up on the intensity of runs, tackles, or winning of second balls when the team are two or three goals down (or up)
- Feign injury, look to pass blame, or try to divert sympathy towards themselves

Fig 3.1.2: Characteristics of players with poor levels of commitment

Commitment: The fundamental knowledge required

The young player who demonstrates these core commitment behaviours does so because they are motivated in specific ways and hold particular beliefs about success and achievement in football. When coaches understand how the quality of motivation drives these commitment behaviours, they hold the key to unlocking an environment that will help players to flourish. Given the integral nature of commitment to the 5Cs process, we will focus on this 'C' with a depth of detail appropriate to its significance.

Intrinsic Motivation and Three Basic Human Needs

To help you grasp what we mean by the quality of motivation, we want you to think about an activity, sport, hobby or role that is passionate to you; that you would want to engage in (or still engage in) without reward, status, or money; that would bring you a sense of enjoyment, happiness or fulfilment. Close your eyes and take a minute to imagine this activity, sport, hobby or role.

If the science is true, then the activity you have selected is very intrinsically motivating to you (i.e., engaging in the activity is inherently satisfying and reward enough on its own).

- It is an activity that you choose to do of your own free will, and no-one is coercing you or pushing you around, forcing you to participate. Moreover, with this choice and free will, the decisions are down to you.
- It is an activity which makes you feel good because you perceive yourself to be good at it, and you draw a sense of competence from your involvement with the activity.
- It is most probably an activity which gives you a sense of social belonging or connectivity with others, where you gain a clear sense that people value and care for you and value the contributions that you make through doing the activity.

When human beings in any walk of life engage in an activity that breeds and nurtures this sense of **autonomy, competence, and relatedness**, then they are likely to devote and sustain intrinsic energy to the activity. These intrinsic energies are often manifested in the core commitment behaviours previously described – human beings passionately commit long hours, mentally focused on the task, without any external reward, challenging themselves and persisting in the process of learning.

In contrast, imagine for a moment a job that you had in the past, or an activity, that did not meet these **three basic human needs**. You were told what to do and had to do the activity (low autonomy/high control), felt or were made to feel incompetent compared to others (low competence), and were left isolated, devalued, uncared for, and disconnected (low relatedness). It's hardly a motivating or fulfilling situation to be in! You certainly aren't going to bust a gut or go the extra mile and, even if the activity was paid well or heightened your status (extrinsic motivation), your lack of ownership disengages you from any meaningful or sustainable thrust to consistently improve yourself.

 **Coaches will influence a player's commitment by helping to nurture their sense of autonomy, competence and relatedness through football.**

These key points are important for coaches with respect to shaping commitment behaviours in young players (indeed any player). Players' commitment levels in football are optimised when playing football is their choice (not their parents), when they feel a sense of competence and progress, and when they feel a sense of affiliation and belonging with others.

There are, nevertheless, a few additional elements that coaches need to consider in competitive football that do not factor into other intrinsic hobbies that are more recreational and non-competitive. This relates to the way in which **competence** is defined by the young player in **competitive** sport.

Task-Orientation and the Growth Mindset

On a Sunday morning anywhere in the country, you might find an Under 9's game happening closely in parallel to an Under 12's game. In terms of these players' behaviours and responses to positive and negative game events, these two age groups are in completely different developmental worlds.

The 8 year olds are running ragged, losing the ball, regaining the ball, falling over, getting back up, and shouting for the ball even when they are nowhere near it. A goal is scored, there is some cheer (mainly from parents), but the losing team get back on with it quickly, and the running starts all over again, until the final whistle blows.

The 11 year olds are more organised, trying to execute a plan which leads to both positive and negative communication to others. Negative body language, anger, and despondency seep onto this pitch a little more when things go against these players. Moreover, a consistency of high effort, regardless of the scoreline or time remaining, is no longer assured in all players compared with the Under 9's match.

What has happened in these three years!?

The answer lies in the cognitive development of the child, and the growing child's ability to interpret information about themselves and their environment. Until 11 years of age (or thereabouts), children lack the cognitive skill to differentiate between their current physical ability and their effort levels as the reasons for their success or failure at football tasks. When Under 9 players are learning a new skill and making mistakes, many of them will see greater or continued effort as a key solution. If another player beats them on a certain drill, makes fewer mistakes, or scores more goals, then they will continue to believe that effort is the key. This effort will make up the difference in the outcomes. Eight- to ten-year-old players may start to see that certain teammates and opponents are somewhat better *right now* on that skill. They may also start to show their disappointment. Nevertheless, they will continue to believe that effort is the answer to developing their skill and ability.

In sum, the cognitive lens of the 8 year old player sees abilities and skills as improvable and learnable through effort. Feelings of competence and ability stem from trying hard and gaining a sense of mastery and self-improvement on a skill. This is essentially why Under 9 players 'get on with it' and tend not to react in an overemotional manner. **They believe in their future by engaging effort in the present.**

Developments in the cognitive spheres of the brain, however, mean that children begin to lose this highly **functional and productive innocence**. By 11 years old, children begin to reason more intelligently and they grasp that ability and effort are very distinct concepts. Children at this stage understand that difficult tasks or skills are those that only a few can perform, and that one's ability (as opposed to effort) can determine whether such tasks are completed.

Effort and ability can indeed become inversely related in the world of an 11 year old. A child may see that ability is actually a fixed capacity that sets the limit upon what effort alone can accomplish. Exerting high effort is simply not enough for an individual to feel successful or competent. Indeed, exerting such high effort can be seen to be an indicator of low ability if one fails at the skill. Children do not want to risk this embarrassment in front of important peers, meaning that some children start to shy away from trying hard in order to protect their self-esteem.

When children achieve this more mature understanding of ability, it is not surprising that we see more avoidance of challenges or trying of new skills, more self-protection, and hiding from the action through fear of failure. Pound for pound, we see less commitment behaviour. Children naturally start to compare their 'ability' with their peers, and become preoccupied with these comparisons as opposed to focusing on their own self-improvement. The need to 'prove' rather than 'improve' can dominate a player's approach to matches and training, whereby mistakes and errors serve as **immediate** indicators that this player is not proving his ability **right here, right now**, compared to others (and indeed to others such as coaches and parents).

A further naturally problematic issue is that whilst the child's cognitive reasoning skills have matured somewhat, they are nowhere near fully mature. An 11 year old male player, for example, will not naturally understand the **relative age effect (i.e. birth dates)** or the concept of **early versus late biological maturation** when measuring himself up against his 'same age group' peers. He may need help to understand that boys could be more able than him now because they are slightly older or bigger at the present time.

Conversely, if he is older and bigger than his peers, he may need help to avoid assuming that his ability is a fixed entity that will make him naturally better than other players **forever**. Indeed, the early maturing boy cannot rest on the laurels of his so-called talent and ability as a pubescent adolescent. In the real world, football will consistently challenge the technical, physical and psychological completeness of the player throughout adolescence and into young adulthood.

Early adolescence is a tough time to be a kid!

Of course, while all children pass through this developmental process and are capable of seeing 'ability' as a product that needs to be continually validated by bettering others, not all children choose to follow this route going forward. Children remain mentally capable of understanding that effort can lead to skill improvements. They can hold onto the belief that ability is a current, changeable characteristic even though they appreciate that others may currently have more of it, and that effort does not automatically guarantee bridging the gap.

When a young player uses this mental lens to interpret and view their current football competence, they are referred to as a player with a high **task orientation**. In line with core commitment behaviours, this child is concerned with the **development** of his or her competence and they use their level of effort and their sense of skill improvement or skill maintenance to appraise their competence in a highly self-versus-self manner. Their current ability is something that is improvable and a sense of satisfaction and achievement stems from their efforts to stretch their pool of skills further.

This belief in the 'improvability' of skills, and the undeterred focus on efforts to get better is sometimes referred to as the **Growth Mindset**[1]. For our purposes in this book, players with a high task orientation are players who carry a growth mindset. In competitive football, where there is such a strong emphasis on proving superior ability (and being positively evaluated and rewarded for such ability), it is vital for youth coaches to continue nourishing and feeding a **Task Orientation** and **Growth Mindset** in their young players. Note again – It is simply vital!

When a coach creates a commitment climate, they help players to develop a task orientation, and to value a personal mindset of improving their skills through effort.

---

[1] Carol Dweck, Mindset: The new psychology for success, Random House, 2006

Commitment coaching: Developing optimally motivated players

The English FA's Future Game document stresses the importance of developing the correct learning **environment** for young players. When we refer to 'commitment coaching', we are taking the three basic psychological needs (competence, autonomy and relatedness) and the task orientation/growth mindset and saying 'Coach in a way that stimulates and nurtures these characteristics'. We are asking coaches to take responsibility for coaching behaviour that grows a task orientation in players, that increases their ownership and decision making skills, and that makes them feel competent and supported. Coaches can take this responsibility every time they interact with a player – before, during, and after training and matches.

In sport psychology, the environment that coaches create to positively influence the quality of motivation and commitment of players is called the **motivational climate.** In this book, the term 'Climate' means 'Environment' because the coach can create Climates or Environments that aren't merely focused on motivation or commitment. You can create a climate or environment that helps nurture the other four 'Cs' as well.

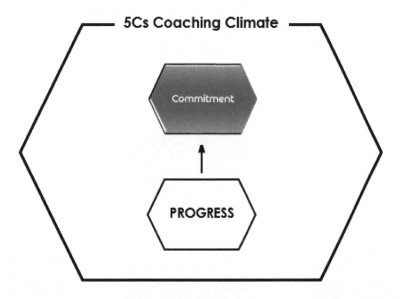

Fig. 3.2: Coaches can create a coaching climate inclusive of all the Cs, underpinned by the PROGRESS behaviours demonstrated by the coach. Commitment is central to the 5Cs climate as it drives the psychological development of the player. This diagram will be developed over the subsequent chapters to reflect the integrative nature of a 5Cs climate.

It is also important to note that the climate created across all 'Cs' extends beyond simply the coach-player dynamic. Other influences, such as parents and peers, are crucial but often not considered a priority. However, the level of influence and dissemination of knowledge about the 5Cs should sensibly extend to those most able to affect the behaviour of the young footballer. The more interest, support, and encouragement that is given by parents (and peers), the more likely it is that the child will acquire positive 5C behaviours, as well as remain involved in football for a long time.

Creating a commitment climate in training

Many of the following ideas may not be new to coaches, because coaching textbooks and courses often suggest behaviours that are meant to motivate and encourage players. Coaches need to take a multidimensional approach to structuring their coaching climate in training and we hope that the ideas presented here reinforce existing elements of your coaching with young players. We also don't expect coaches to work through the list of behaviours and strategies in a strictly linear fashion. Our advice is that you integrate some behaviours and strategies purposefully in your coaching sessions, perhaps as part of a session plan. Other behaviours and strategies may be reactive or spontaneous according to what has happened in the session. Over time, if you pay attention to your behaviour in sessions, and reflect after your sessions, your commitment coaching skills will become more refined and automatic.

The starting point, of course, is that players begin to understand your 'commitment values' as a coach so that **their behaviour** becomes aligned to **your values**. Remember that to produce the **four core commitment behaviours**, the values of effort, skill learning, personal improvement, autonomy, and social support will form the fabric of the commitment coaching climate.

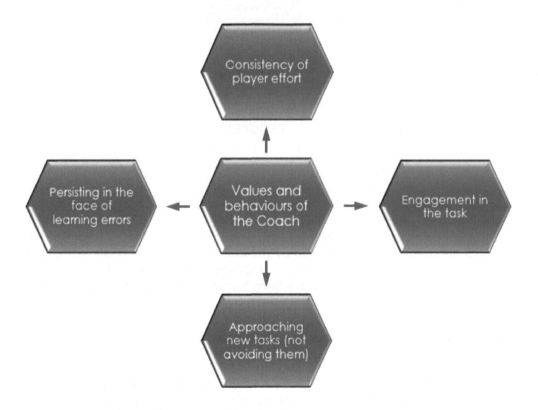

Fig 3.3: How much you value and demonstrate the four commitment behaviours will reflect on how much your player's value and demonstrate them consistently in training and matches.

Commitment: Coaching practices

A committed player is one who approaches a training session with the same mental readiness and structure as they would for a cup final, or some other important match. They would go into it knowing exactly what they want to get out of that session and how they are going to go about getting it. How well a player focuses on using training sessions to make personal improvement will determine how productive that training session actually is. At the top level of the game, players always do more than just enough. They are always searching for how they can do better, since where they are now will not be good enough for tomorrow.

This also rings true of high level coaches who are constantly demonstrating and transmitting their commitment values onto the players and onto the pitch. A large part of this will include how your coaching behaviours 'PROGRESS' commitment throughout your session. The practices ahead show examples and provide reminders of how you can emphasise the principles of 'PROGRESS' (see Chapter 2) from the start of the session to introduce, or *promote,* commitment - through to the end of the session in order to debrief, or allow for the players to *self-review* how committed they were during the session. 'Coachable' moments don't just occur during the practices you put on for the players. So the time available pre and post-training gives you an invaluable opportunity to effectively introduce and close down your player's learning.

The opportunity to demonstrate each of the eight coaching behaviours of 'PROGRESS' is present within every training session. The skill of the coach will, for example, be in artfully selecting the appropriate moments to *reinforce* a player's committed behaviour, or in identifying the opportunity to *praise* a player who has *supported his teammates.* Therefore the purpose of this section is to reinforce the idea of 'PROGRESS' through a range of practices, strategies, and behaviours that are aimed at helping you to transmit your values around commitment during your coaching practices.

Each example practice is structured in three parts. The first part shows the layout of the drill and explains how to set it up and how to organise the practice. The second part describes possible strategies and tasks you can implement in order to 'add in' and emphasise the commitment behaviours you desire from your group of players. Some of these strategies and behaviours are better suited to the 'Foundation Phase' player (8-11 age range), whilst others are more developmentally appropriate to the 'Youth Development Phase' player (12-16 age range). The third part acts as a reminder of the 'PROGRESS' coaching behaviours and runs down the side of the 'C' strategies. Where the strategies we use are reflective of an element of 'PROGRESS' we highlight the relevant coach behaviour. In doing so you will appreciate the variety of ways in which commitment can be influenced within any given practice and in any given training session.

The strategies and behaviours we show within each practice are merely examples and not tied to the practice itself. We encourage you to select the most appropriate strategy from our examples, or create your own to meet the commitment (and wider 5Cs) needs of your players. As such, at the end of the chapter we will summarise the strategies and behaviours used within the practices and indicate which are best suited for use with younger players, and which are more appropriate for adolescent players.

Based on the F.A. Future Game manual the practices themselves are a mixture of warm-ups, main session exercises and small sided games. These practices provide you with real-world examples of how you can 'add in' and emphasise commitment coaching within your training sessions. We also provide practical examples of how you might go about setting up your commitment behaviours pre-session, as well as how you may conduct a post-session debrief in order to review your players' commitment behaviours.

Commitment
Coaching practices

Practice	Part of the Session				Development Phase	
	Pre Session	Warm Up	Main Session	Post Session	5-11	12-16
Taking Aim	●	○	○	○	●	●
King of the Road	○	●	○	○	●	○
Trigger	○	●	○	○	●	○
Pass and Move	○	●	○	○	○	●
Tag Game with Corner Boxes	○	●	○	○	○	●
Dribbling and Ball Manipulation	○	○	●	○	●	●
Risky Business	○	○	●	○	●	○
Breakout Game	○	○	●	○	○	●
2v2 Shooting	○	○	●	○	○	●
Before You Leave...	○	○	○	●	●	●

Key:

○   Does not relate to this part of the session/not appropriate for this age group

●   Relates to this part of the session/appropriate for this age group

Chapter 3

P romote

R ole model

O wnership

G row

R einforce

E mpower

S upport
supporter

S elf-review

Session Purpose

- Draw the player's attention to the value and importance of commitment
- Begin to focus the player's thoughts on the upcoming session
- Give each player the opportunity to contribute through group discussions and allowing time for feedback
- Provide the chance for the players to interact with each other in a non-threatening environment
- Start to give the players ownership over their learning by allowing the players to lead discussions and the task

To Introduce Commitment

To develop a committed player by setting clear goals related to responses the player wants to demonstrate in training.

Organisation: When working with younger players, or players who are learning to develop their goal-setting skills, try the following exercise at the beginning of training. Ask a few players to tell you and the rest of the team about two or three mental and technical skills they want to focus on in the session. What do they want to focus on achieving as players? You may wish to start with yourself and share with the players the mental skills you are going to work on as the coach?

You need not do this for every player, every session, but ensure that you work around the whole team during the week, asking a few to speak up. This will then get the rest of the team talking and sharing information about their own goals. When everybody appreciates what everybody else is working on personally or wanting to achieve from a session, it can improve the quality and direction of the training.

You may wish to progress this by asking the players to write down their goals for each session and begin to keep a weekly diary.

Review: Gather the group together at the end of the session. Ask the players who publicly set mental and technical goals at the start of the session to quickly review how successful they were in achieving each of their goals. You can also ask them what they think they need to continue focusing on in the next session. By reaffirming these player's new targets at the start of the next session, and asking new players to volunteer their personal goals for the session, you will quickly develop a shared sense of purpose in training tends to elevate levels of motivation. This means higher energy, persistence and productivity. Consequently the team will start to work for each other to a much higher level than if this understanding was not gained.

44

King of the Road

To Add and Emphasise Commitment

P romote

Player Ownership: To develop a sense of autonomy and give the player's a sense of ownership, give each team four footballs. The players choose whether they wish to attack 1v1 (award 4 points for a successful attempt), 2v1 (3 points), 3v1 (2 points) or 4v1 (1 point)

R ole model

O wnership

Setting a Goal: To promote the player's engagement in the task and encourage them to approach new challenges, ask them to set a number of goals they think they can score out of four. Can they achieve that goal?

G row

Sweat 'o' Meter: To encourage physical and mental effort in the practice, stop the practice and use the idea of a sweat 'o' meter to gauge the efforts of the players. Ask each team to rate their efforts so far (how much they are 'sweating') based upon football clubs in the league. For example the yellow team may think they are 'sweating as hard as Liverpool'. Ask for a reason why they think that, and ask them what team they would want to be in the next 10 minutes in terms of showing higher mental and physical effort. For example, the yellow team may set themselves the target of 'sweating like Manchester United' as being an improvement on Liverpool!

R einforce

E mpower support

S upport supporter

S elf-review

Practice Set Up

- Set up a pitch of an appropriate size for the number and age of the players
- Arrange eight 'mini gates' as shown in the diagram above
- Organise three teams of four players: four blue guards and two teams of four attackers
- The four blue 'guards' defend two of the mini gates each
- The red and yellow players stand on each side of the grid with four cones
- The red players attack the top blue guards, and the yellow players attack the bottom two blue guards

Practice Organisation

- When the coach shouts "Go!" the first red and yellow players pick up a cone and choose which of their two goals to attack
- The aim is for the red and yellow players to get past the blue guard, run through one of the two gates and put their cone down behind the gate
- If the red and yellow players achieve this they score 1 point for their team
- The blue guards get a point each time they 'tag' the attacking player
- At that point the attacking player drops their cone and joins the back of their line
- Each player takes it in turns to attack the guards and the winner is the team with the most points (cones through the gates) at the end of four attacks

Chapter 3

P romote	
R ole model	
O wnership	
G row	
R einforce	
E mpower support	
S upport supporter	
S elf-review	

To Add and Emphasise Commitment

Which Pitch? To draw the player's attention to the value of physical and mental effort, give them the choice of which pitch (or part of the pitch) they are ready to train on. Pitch 1 is for players who are ready to train with a Premiership level of effort; Pitch 2 is for players who want to work at a Championship level etc. What pitch are you ready to train on today? Use this as a motivational reminder during the session if you feel that players are not paying attention, or giving the appropriate level of effort. You can bring players down to a 'lower level' and set them the goal of earning their way back up to the higher level pitch. You can also hand ownership over to the squad, and let them tell you when they feel they have earned the 'transfer'. Just make sure they give you a reason as well!

Personalised Feedback: To ensure the players feel a sense of ownership over their performance/improvements, give specific feedback to each player. Reward them for the effort they have put into to make improvements and personalise it by using their first name (or nickname)

Practice Set Up

- Set up a practice area of 25 yards x 25 yards for three teams of five players as shown above
- The size of the area can be amended as necessary according to the age and ability of the players in the group
- To begin the practice ask the players to move freely around the area

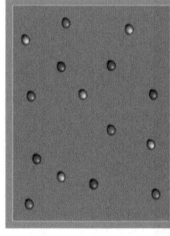

Practice Organisation

- One team is designated as the 'trigger' group and is given a 'trigger' movement (for example: hopping, skipping, side-stepping, running backwards)
- The other two teams are given a movement to perform in response to the trigger group
- At any time a nominated player in the 'trigger' group can 'trigger' the activity by performing their movement
- For example, the trigger group runs fast weaving in and out of the other two groups, while the remaining groups balance on one leg.
- The coach changes the activities for each group and changes the 'trigger' practice

46

Pass and Move

Warm Up Exercise

To Add and Emphasise Commitment

P romote

Appraise Effort: To encourage physical and mental effort from the player's stop the practice and ask the players how much effort they think they are showing on a scale 1 (no effort) to 10 (maximum effort). Why do they think that and what can they do to raise their level of effort for the rest of the practice?

R ole model

O wnership

Stepping it Up: To encourage the players to approach new challenges, have the players move the ball between the target players in different ways, such as:

- Only using their stronger/weaker foot
- Keeping the ball off the ground
- Only using their heads
- Only using 1 touch per person

G row

R einforce

Group Collaboration: To foster relatedness and increase engagement on the task between attempts, ask the players to discuss and come up with one or two improvements they could make as a group to improve their movement of the ball between each of the target players

E mpower support

S upport supporter

S elf-review

Practice Set Up

- Organise a pitch of 25 yards x 15 yards
- Set up four small 'target' boxes in the corners of the pitch
- Split the group into three teams of four
- One group of four is positioned in the target boxes (yellow)
- The remaining groups of four (red and blue) spread themselves out in the middle of the grid
- Each of the middle groups have a football each

Practice Organisation

- The middle red and blue teams look to pass the ball between them
- The aim is to pass the ball into a yellow target player in each corner until they have passed the ball to all four corners
- Each player must touch the ball before it is played into a corner
- The teams can pass into the corners in any order they wish
- Both groups are aiming to do this faster than the other group

47

Chapter 3

Warm Up Exercise

To Add and Emphasise Commitment

P romote

R ole model

O wnership

G row

R einforce

E mpower
support

S upport
supporter

S elf-review

Player Ownership: To develop autonomy and give the players a sense of ownership, allow the players to choose a skill or activity they feel they wish to work on, or improve in each of the corner boxes

Appraise Effort: To encourage physical and mental effort during the task, stop the practice and ask the 'taggers' how much effort they think they are showing on a scale 1 (no effort) to 10 (maximum effort). Can they raise their effort levels?

Setting a Goal: To promote engagement in the task and encourage the players to approach new challenges, each player is given a football. At the end of each round ask the players to come up with ways they can improve their performance to avoid being tagged. For example, using body feints or changes of direction/turns

Practice Set Up

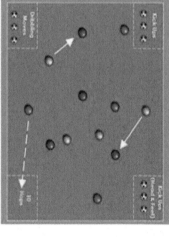

- Set up an area of 25 yards x 25 yards is organised with four corner boxes marked as shown in the diagram
- Amend the size of the area as necessary according to the age and ability of the players in the group
- Organise three teams of four players, with one team designated as the 'tagging' team (in the diagram above the yellow team has been designated the 'tagging' team)
- The practice starts in the central area

Practice Organisation

- The tagging team are given 60 seconds to try and tag as many players as possible
- If a player is tagged, they must go to one of the squares and perform the designated activity
- Once completed they can re-join the practice
- Swap the tagging team over after 60 seconds
- The challenge for the tagging team is to see if they can send every attacker to one of the activity squares in 60 seconds

Dribbling and Ball Manipulation

Main Session Exercise

To Add and Emphasise Commitment

P romote

Setting a Goal: To promote engagement in the task and encourage the players to approach new challenges, challenge the players:

- How many successful attempts can the player make?
- How many successful and consecutive attempts can the player make?
- Can they beat their own personal scores?

R ole model

O wnership

Stepping It Up: Encourage the players to approach new challenges by increasing the difficulty of the practice. For example, ask them to use their weaker foot, or introduce 'blockers' into the practice who dribble a ball and attempt to stop players from going to/dribbling through a gate

G row

R einforce

Personalised Feedback: To ensure the players feel a sense of ownership over their performance/improvements, give specific feedback to each player. Reward them for the effort they have put into make improvements and personalise it by using their first name (or nickname)

E mpower support

S upport supporter

S elf-review

Practice Set Up

- Organise an appropriate sized area for the age and number of players in the group
- Set up a number of 'gates' around the area, as shown in the diagram above
- Each player should have a ball
- The coach challenges the players to perform various exercises/skills at eac gate, for example:
  - Dribble through all of the gates
  - Dribble a 'figure of 8' around the two cones
  - Perform a turn at each gate
  - Move through the gates performing kick-ups
  - Tap the ball between both feet when travelling through a gate

Practice Organisation

- Each time a player successfully performs the skill they shout "Yes"
- Each time a player feels they can perform the skill better, they shout "Better"
- When the majority of the players are able to shout "Yes", introduce a new skill for the players to perform
- Each new skill introduced should be progressively more difficult than the previous one
- When introducing a new skill, provide the players with an 'opt-out' option, which they can use once during the practice
- This 'opt-out' allows the player to continue practicing a skill that they

Chapter 3

Main Session Exercise

P romote

R ole model

O wnership

G row

R einforce

E mpower support

S upport supporter

S elf-review

To Add and Emphasise Commitment

Player Ownership: To develop autonomy and give the players a sense of ownership allow the players to choose how they attack (1v1, 2v1, 3v2 or 4v2)

Setting a Goal: To promote engagement in the task and encourage the players to approach new challenges, ask the players to set themselves a target number of points they wish to achieve

Stepping it Up: To encourage the players to approach new challenges, increase the challenge to the players by adding additional attackers and defenders

Sweat 'o' Meter: To encourage physical and mental effort in the practice, stop the practice and use the idea of a sweat 'o' meter to gauge the efforts of the players. Ask each team to rate their efforts so far (how much they are 'sweating') based upon football clubs in the league. Ask for a reason why they think that, and ask them what team they would want to be in the next 10 minutes in terms of showing higher mental and physical effort.

Practice Set Up

- Set up a pitch approximately 40 yards x 15 yards with a half way line marked
- Organise two equal teams one defending (red) and one attacking (blue), plus two goalkeepers
- The defending team is divided equally to defend each goal
- The attacking team begin the practice at the half way line and off the pitch
- The practice starts with the first attacking player dribbling the ball into either half to attack one of the goals

Practice Organisation

- The attacking team have as many footballs as there will be attacks (e.g. 5 footballs for 5 attacks)
- The blues can attack in the following ways: 1v1 and receive 5 points per goal; 2v1 and receive 2 points per goal; 3v2 and receive 4 points per goal; 4v2 and receive 3 points per goal
- For each goal scored, the same players turn and attack the goal at the other end
- If they keep scoring, they keep attacking each goal
- If they miss or if the defenders win possession and pass to the coach, that attack is over and the next ball is used

Breakout Game

To Add and Emphasise Commitment

P romote

'Future-Proof' Coaching: To help foster persistence amongst the players, help your players prepare for and accept learning errors by asking the players: **"When** you find it more difficult to...**then**, what do you think the best response would be from a committed player/your role model?" This way you lessen any of the player's fear about 'what to do when....'

R ole model

O wnership

Team Work: To foster relatedness and increase engagement on the task, ask the players to evaluate the team performance and come up with ways to make improvements.

G row

Stepping It Up: To encourage the players to approach new challenges, increase the difficulty by allowing the initial defender to recover and defend in the final third. The attacker now has to finish under the pressure of less time and space. Alternatively, allow the initial defender to recover to the middle third creating a 1v2 situation

R einforce

E mpower
support

Appraise Effort: To encourage physical and mental effort in the practice, stop the practice and ask the players how much effort they think they are showing on a scale 1 (no effort) to 10 (maximum effort). Why do they think that and what can they do raise their effort levels for the rest of the practice?

S upport
supporter

S elf-review

Practice Set Up

- Set up an area of 30 yards x10 yards with goals at each end
- The size of the area can be amended as necessary according to the age and ability of the players in the group
- Two teams of three players

Practice Organisation

- The practice starts with the red attackers in their defensive zone
- The red attacking team play 3v1 against the blue defender to release 1 player into the middle zone
- The red attacker then plays 1v1 against a blue defender in the middle zone
- The third blue defender becomes the goalkeeper
- The red attacker looks to beat the defender 1v1 in the middle zone and then go to score in the attacking zone
- After 6 sets, rotate the players

51

Chapter 3

Main Session Exercise

P romote	
R ole model	
O wnership	
G row	
R einforce	
E mpower support	
S upport supporter	
S elf-review	

To Add and Emphasise Commitment

Setting a Goal: To promote engagement in the task and encourage the players to approach new challenges, ask the players:

- How many shots do the attackers think they can make out of 10 attacks?
- How many shots on target do the attackers think they can make out of 10 attacks?
- How many goals do the attackers think they can score out of 10 attacks?
- When the attackers achieve the target they set, can they beat it?

Team Work: To foster relatedness and increase engagement on the task ask the players: which areas does the defending team (including the goalkeeper) think they need to work at, and (including the goalkeeper) think they need to work at, and which areas does the attacking team (including the servers) believe they need to improve on to create more shooting/scoring opportunities?

'Future-Proof' Coaching: To help foster persistence amongst the players, help your players prepare for and accept learning errors by asking the players: **"When** you find it more difficult to... **then**, what do you think the best response would be from a committed player/your role model?" This way you lessen any of

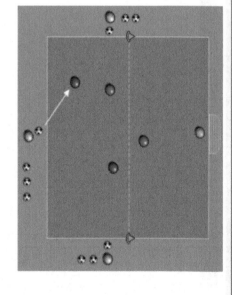

Practice Set Up

- Set up a 20 yards x 20 yards square with an offside line marked out at 10 yards, and a goal at one end
- Arrange 8 players into 2 red attackers, 2 blue defenders, 1 goalkeeper and 3 yellow servers
- 10 footballs are spread around the servers

Practice Organisation

- The practice starts with the 2 red attackers working as a pair, moving to receive the a pass from one of the three servers
- The defenders look to defend against the attackers to prevent a shot at goal
- When the defenders win possession they pass to the nearest server
- Attackers can only be caught offside in the 10 yards nearest to goal
- A new ball is fed in to continue the practice
- At the end of 10 attacks, change the roles of the players

Before You Leave...

Post Session Exercise

Session Purpose

P romote
- To 'close' the session down appropriately
- Work with the players to set a future direction for the next commitment training session
- To collaborate with the player's to review the quality of team commitment strategy use
- Provide the players with the opportunity to self-reflect on their own commitment performance and judge what they

R ole model
have learnt from the training session

To Review Commitment

O wnership
Give the players to opportunity to quickly recap and assess their use of commitment skills and their learning within the session.

Organisation: At the end of the training session notify the players that they will be asked the following two questions before they leave:

- How much did you show that you were a consistently committed players throughout the session?
- What one thing did you learn from the session that you can take into the next training session/match?

G row
Then allow the players a little time to consider their answers to these questions. Prior to leaving each player has to come up to you and give their answers to the two above questions. When hearing the answers from the players you may wish to probe them further to gauge how considered and thoughtful the player's answers are.

R einforce
At the start of the next session you can ask the players to remember their answers to these questions from the last session. By asking the players to think back to what they learnt from the previous session and how well they performed, you quickly tie the current session into the previous one. Tying sessions in this manner will not only help improve the players learning but also set expectation levels to improve performances in the current session.

E mpower
support

S upport
supporter

S elf-review

Commitment: Summary

Commitment coaching and creating a climate and environment that 'shapes' high quality motivation in young players is as much an art as it is a science. The science can give you these principles, and the art is having the presence of mind to plan not only your commitment strategies, but also to respond to events spontaneously that send a learning message to the individual player and the entire squad. If you've practiced your art well then players as young as eight or nine upwards should be reasonably capable of describing those core commitment behaviours that they and you both value.

You will hopefully notice in these strategies that we have emphasised the value of a task oriented/growth mindset approach to competence. However, you will also see a care to nourish the autonomy of players by giving them options, taking ownership of supporting others, involving them in decisions, and allowing them to make choices. The level of peer and coach support in valuing effort and skill improvement as a very individual journey also helps the player to feel cared for and connected to others.

There will be players that you coach who may have come from a different background or environment (created by other coaches and parents) who may struggle because of their excessive focus on their ability compared to peers, or their fear of making mistakes (i.e., they are fixated on 'proving' rather than 'improving'). These commitment coaching tools can help these players start to turn a corner so long as the wider **commitment climate** is present and strong. Therefore, it is important that you counsel and educate parents and grandparents in your strategies if you begin to see players backing off from the core commitment behaviours that underpin high quality motivation.

Coaching strategies and behaviours summary

Strategy	Targeting Commitment				Development Phase	
	Effort	Engagement	Approach Tasks	Persistence	5-11	12-16
Appraise Effort	●	○	○	●	○	●
Future-Proof Coaching	○	○	●	●	○	●
Group Collaboration	○	●	●	○	○	●
Personalised Feedback	●	●	●	●	●	●
Player Ownership	●	●	●	○	●	●
Setting a Goal	○	●	●	○	●	●
Stepping it Up	●	●	●	○	●	●
Sweat 'o' Meter	●	○	○	●	●	○
Team Work	○	●	●	○	○	●
Which Pitch?	●	●	●	●	●	●

Key:

○   Not the focus of this strategy/not appropriate for this age group

●   Focus of this exercise/appropriate for this age group

4
Communication

The second 'C', fundamental to learning, performance and enjoyment in football, is Communication. Within the FA's four corner model, communication overlaps the psychological and social corners because it is a clear 'psycho-social' attribute. It is an interpersonal skill that dominates social situations, and reflects our ability to relate to another person or persons. The communication process features how information is sent, received and interpreted between two or more people. The quality of this process has psychological effects because it directly impacts on the **thoughts**, **feelings** and subsequent **actions** or **performances** of one, both, or all people involved.

In its simplest terms, within coaching and training sessions, communication by the coach and between players can be:

- **Verbal responses** in the form of specific information, feedback, praise, encouragement or instructions

    Or

- **Non-verbal** behavioural responses (i.e., body or hand signals for a pass; a reaction of dismay to a player's mistake; a positive or negative gesture to a teammate; the visual demonstration of a skill or technique to players by a coach)

Non-verbal responses also include actions, decisions or behaviours that represent what one person thinks or feels about another person. For example, events such as: non-selection for the team; not passing the ball to a teammate who is the best option; or a player turning his back on someone and walking off when he is being talked to. These are all forms of communication, and not pleasant ones in these instances.

Chapter 4

All verbal and non-verbal communications send messages to the '**receiving**' player and often this is related to what the '**sender**' thinks of them or their behaviour. Obviously some of these messages can be a lot more positive and motivational than others! Effective communication is based on all players (and staff) sending *positive* and/or *constructive* information and *receiving* and *processing* this information to help individual and team performance. Like text messaging, the one truth about communication is that once a message is sent it can never be recalled or revised. It will be interpreted by the receiver in a certain way and sometimes misinterpreted.

 **Make time as a coach to focus on the development of your players' communication skills – both verbal and non-verbal, and in varying contexts (e.g., pre-match, training, match, post-match).**

Communication is the second 'C' in the 5C framework because it is a significant psycho-social skill for young players to master not only because football is a team sport, but because football players generally interact with so many different types of people in their lives. Communication skills influence team and individual performances and they need to be performed effectively to have an influence. Indeed, when we consider many youth teams and individuals in football, communication is probably **one of the most underperformed skills** compared to its potential impact on well-being, motivation and performance. Therefore, the role of the coach is not only focused on helping players to talk and share information and encouragement, it also centres upon helping players to accept and use constructive feedback for positive gains.

As with the first 'C', Commitment, take a moment to consider the behaviours that you would wish to see in a player with excellent **communication skills.** What would be the key characteristics and behaviours that you would pick out? What would you ideally expect of the specific age group that you are working with? Having done this you may wish to consider what the opposite list might look like. What does poor, detrimental or harmful communication look like? As with commitment, your own age group will be made up of players who show a wide range of communication-related abilities dependent upon their stage of development.

Depending on whether you are discussing Under 10 players or Under 16 players, the specific expectations and current capabilities will be very different. However, if you do this exercise, you will now have more of a reflective blueprint of what you would like to promote within your coaching that you might have targeted less before.

Below is an example of a list developed by coaches in a professional club when reflecting on senior players. Can you help your players to establish the core foundations of communication such that they become consistently excellent communicators when they are young adult players?

A player with excellent communication will...

- Give information and instruction to teammates with respect to space, time and decision-making options
- Support and encourage teammates after a mistake or when they are facing a tough personal battle
- Listen to teammates' instructions with respect and make considered decisions
- Praise and positively reinforce teammates in response to their efforts or skill
- Give positive, constructive criticism to players after a move has broken down or state what they need to do more of
- Encourage and raise the intensity of the team when momentum is in their favour
- Manage their frustration at a teammate or event by encouraging what they can do next, not what they've just failed to do
- Show appreciation for a teammate's efforts and acknowledge the intention behind their decision
- Ask questions of the coach to further their own understanding
- Seek clarification from the coach when they don't understand something
- Pay attention to the coach and take on-board the information the coach gives

Fig 4.1.1: Characteristics of players with excellent levels of communication

A player with poor communication will...

- Stay quiet and give no information to teammates about positioning or time pressure
- Fail to inform teammates of threats or fail to guide players to positive decisions that they can see
- Fail to give praise and reinforcement to a teammate who has done something well, particularly after being critical of him earlier
- Blatantly ignore a teammate's valid instructions
- Blame/criticise teammates in front of others for poor execution when effort and intention were actually excellent from that player
- Show negative body language and/or verbal criticism to a teammate after a move didn't come off, without considering the other options or decisions that the player had to face
- Stay quiet and not seek to ask questions, seek clarification or interact with the coach
- Ignore input from the coach, or need points repeating

Fig 4.1.2: Characteristics of players with poor levels of communication

Communication: The fundamental knowledge required

Communication skills (both verbal and non-verbal) need to be practiced consistently both on and off the pitch. Opportunities for practicing positive communication and effective interactions with teammates lie everywhere. If these opportunities are consistently taken then you begin to build an exceptionally self-aware team of individuals who begin to understand the current strengths and limitations of others... and work together to enhance their collective performances.

In terms of core knowledge for coaches, we have coined the acronym **'HELPA'** to serve as a useful reminder when working with young players and shaping their interpersonal foundations at every turn. It is relevant to all ages of player, and once players understand what each letter of HELPA means then you need only to ask questions that challenge the degree to which players felt that they were **effective HELPAs** in a given situation.

HELPA stands for:

- **H**elp
- **E**ncourage
- **L**isten
- **P**raise
- **A**cknowledge (or **A**ccept)

Let's take a brief look at what each of these words mean in order to help your education to players as a communication coach.

Help

'Help' represents the instructional aspect of player-to-player and coach-to-player communication, with a focus on more **direct instructions and information** to help a player's learning, positioning, decision making, and support role. This is the most prevalent form of ongoing communication that we may see on the pitch. The role of the coach is to educate players in the value of 'helping' commands (e.g., time; man on), instructions, and 'time-constrained' requests. A key responsibility of the coach therefore lies in monitoring the quality of the 'helping' that players offer as well as ensuring that players appreciate how direct commands are sent for **performance reasons** and are not meant as **personal criticism**. The coach's role is also to help empower quieter players in asserting themselves (e.g., giving them the responsibility as leaders in their units, and making small, gradual improvements in commands).

Encourage

On-pitch encouragement that serves to inspire, intensify effort, and empower confidence is a communication behaviour that can tie together all of the 5C's, bringing greater concentration and self-control to teams. Asking or discussing with players about when the best times to encourage are (e.g., after mistakes; after a specific game event; when entering a crucial period of the game etc.), and what to encourage, can help the coach and players to create agreed 'communication goals' for training sessions and matches.

Chapter 4

Listen

Listening is an attentional skill, and a life skill, that demands not only concentration and hearing ability but interpretation skills as well. The effective listening player processes the information given, sometimes in the face of competing information and noise. Depending on the nature of the information, this process may trigger positive and negative thoughts, images and feelings, culminating in actions or behaviour as a result of the information. For our purposes, listening skills are about **readiness to receive information** from the coach and from fellow players. It is about creating a value amongst players that it is respectful to listen, to pay attention, and to allow players to 'help' you out or offer feedback. Coaches can help players to practice their listening skills in training by setting up drills that demand this between players, from coach-to–player, and importantly, from player-to-coach.

Praise

Praising is the more concrete and specific 'brother' or 'sister' to 'Encouragement'. Whilst players might offer encouragement more fluidly and dynamically through game situations and challenging periods of play, praise tends to be connected to a specific event (massive tackle; huge save; excellent run and attempt on goal). Once again, the effects of praise have positive effects on motivation and confidence as well as team cohesion and social belonging (i.e., who wants to be part of a team where you don't get any praise!). However be careful not to 'over praise' players, or teammates, as doing so can lessen its impact and devalue it in the eyes of the player. In essence, they may 'tune-out' to your praise.

Sometimes praise between players (and from coaches) can occur after games and in off-pitch settings; and a role of the coach is to help engender an environment where praise is appropriate and a natural part of a training session and match. For young players, being set the goal of appropriately praising different teammates during or after a match can help them to establish their confidence, their relationships, and the inherent moral value in supporting another player/peer.

Coaching players to be excellent communicators fosters 'relatedness' in a team which, as you know, has important effects on the Commitment and motivation of players.

Acknowledge and Accept

Whereas helping, encouraging and praising are 'sending' skills, listening and acknowledging/accepting are 'receiving' skills. 'Acknowledging' on the pitch is often a non-verbal physical gesture (i.e., a clap or thumbs up for trying to find the player with a pass) reflective of the effort or intention of the teammate. It can also encompass listening to a teammate's point of view, and then being appreciative of their position, opinion, or feedback to the player. When a poor decision has been made, or an action has occurred that has negatively affected a teammate, this feedback can often be critical and emotional in the heat of the moment. The mental strength of a player to take responsibility for his actions (and learn from them) lie - to begin with - in his ability to acknowledge and accept the nature of the information that is being communicated to him.

Accepting that it is a fellow teammate's momentary frustration that is being vented at the player leaves him in much better mental shape than if he was to interpret this teammate's words as a direct and enduring personal attack on his ability. For coaches of older youth players, there will probably be many opportunities to positively and proactively discuss the role of acknowledgement and acceptance, as well as the 'empowering' manner in which information can be given in the first place. When young players begin to master acceptance of other players' emotions, they are automatically strengthening mastery of their own emotions.

In football culture it is important not to discount that many coaches of older youth players believe in the value of harsh communication and emotion-laden, personalised public criticism in an attempt to render the youth player resilient to the effects of such behaviour in the senior game. As authors, we can appreciate the logic and function behind the delivery of such emotional and public feedback to a young player. The art of emotionally toughening players up in this way divides opinion. However, we would maintain that it is important for feedback to focus on the behaviour/action and not the person (e.g., limiting the use of 'You' when addressing the player). Secondly, it is advisable for coaches to ensure that their personal relationship with an individual player is seen as human and caring in nature, and that they inform players about their general communication style and the rationale behind it in their coaching role (i.e., coaches clarify the purpose and goals of their communications). Can you build a caring foundation as a coach from which certain emotional, critical feedback is seen by players in a helping manner? In this respect, when a coach delivers critical feedback of a specific behaviour, he is more able to distance this coaching role-related feedback from the personal relationship he has with a player. When a coach can remove the relationship from the feedback, it is easier for a young player to accept information without the added burden of feeling like their relationship with a coach has been destroyed.

Communication coaching: Developing optimally supportive players

In the same way that we challenge coaches to create a commitment climate within their coaching practice, we similarly encourage them to target their behaviour towards developing the **communication** skills of young players. Once again, coaches can take this responsibility every time they interact with a player – before, during, and after training and matches.

As with the other 'Cs', the learning environment that coaches create to influence the quality of communication can be referred to as the **communication climate.** In promoting the interactions between and within peers, as well as with yourself, you also help to reinforce elements of your commitment climate. You will be providing the opportunities for your players to relate to one another. As you will no doubt see, throughout the remainder of this book, this overlap and interaction between the 'Cs' is a recurring theme!

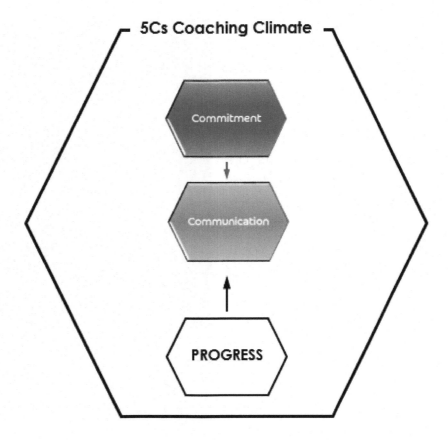

Fig 4.2: Targeting and promoting communication behaviours will create a more open and supportive climate geared towards performance improvement

In building on from the commitment coaching practices presented earlier, the following section directly focuses on strategies and behaviours themed around improving your players' communication skills.

Communication: Coaching practices

Developing and actively practicing good communication skills with teammates is seldom a specifically targeted objective within a football training session. How well a team communicates with each member will have a genuine effect on the responses and behaviour of each individual. Simply because a player is talking a lot doesn't necessarily mean that they are an effective communicator! Communication is therefore a major skill that you and your players should actively seek to improve in every training session.

Chapter 4

Using the strategies and behaviours outlined in the following pages, together with your commitment strategies, you can begin to create a 'toolbox' of methods to accentuate communication. As before, some of these strategies and behaviours are better suited to the 'Foundation Phase' player (8-11 age range), whilst others are more developmentally appropriate to the 'Youth Development Phase' player (12-16 age range), as indicated in the practice. Our advice is that you attempt to integrate these communication principles in your coaching sessions initially by *promoting* the value of effective communication between your players, and by working with them to identify positive *role* models of communication. Some of your other 'PROGRESS' coaching behaviours may be reactive or spontaneous according to what has happened in the session. As with the commitment practices, some of the example strategies we provide are reflective of particular behaviours of the 'PROGRESS' acronym.

Over the following pages we present examples of how to develop effective communication skills and behaviours that are inclusive of the pre-session period and post-session debrief. The main session practices are again a mixture of warm-ups, main session exercises, and small sided games. In order to build upon the foundations established with your commitment coaching, the warm-up exercises are the same as those from the previous Commitment section. We have retained example commitment strategies within the practice in order to continue reinforcing your player's commitment behaviours, whilst adding and integrating more robust communication strategies as detailed in the practices. It is left to the discretion of the coach whether they feel it necessary to overtly draw their players' attention to the prior commitment-related behaviours, or focus solely on developing their communication skills. At the end of the chapter, we will once more summarise the strategies and behaviours used within the practices and indicate which are best suited for use with younger and older players.

Communication
Coaching practices

Practice	Part of the Session				Development Phase	
	Pre Session	Warm Up	Main Session	Post Session	5-11	12-16
Communication Role Models	●	○	○	○	●	●
King of the Road	○	●	○	○	●	○
Trigger	○	●	○	○	●	○
Pass and Move	○	●	○	○	○	●
Tag Game with Corner Boxes	○	●	○	○	○	●
Passing and Support Play	○	○	●	○	●	○
Support Play	○	○	●	○	●	○
Communication Focused Match	○	○	●	○	○	●
Defending as a Defensive Unit	○	○	●	○	○	●
Divide and Conquer	○	○	○	●	●	●

Key:
- ○ Does not relate to this part of the session/not appropriate for this age group
- ● Relates to this part of the session/appropriate for this age group

Chapter 4

P romote	
R ole model	
O wnership	
G row	
R einforce	
E mpower	
S upport	
S upporter	
S elf-review	

Session Purpose

- Draw the player's attention to the value and importance of communication
- Begin to focus the player's thoughts on the upcoming session
- Give each player the opportunity to contribute through group discussions and allowing time for feedback
- Provide the chance for the players to interact with each other in a non-threatening environment
- Start to give the players ownership over their learning by allowing the players to lead discussions and the task

To Introduce Communication

To raise the player's awareness of the importance of communication.

Organisation: Begin by discussing with the players that communication skills influence team and individual performances and so they need to be performed effectively. Fortunately good communication is something that can improved if they want to, but it is not simply a case of saying something, or anything to anyone. Let them know that good communication is the art of sending and receiving information that exists between two or more people. The quality of this process has an impact on the thoughts, feelings and actions or performance of one, both or all people involved.

Group the players into threes or fours. Each group is tasked with selecting their starting team of excellent 'role model' communicators. It may be useful to provide the players with the ability to write down their answers. Ask the players to:

- Select a formation that they wish to play (for 11-a-side, 9-a-side or 7-a-side)
- For each position they need to choose a player who plays in the professional game, who they think is an excellent communicator
- For each player they need provide two or three reasons/behaviours that they feel shows that their chosen player is an excellent communicator (e.g. gives lots of good, specific information)
- Having selected a team and justified their selections, the group should now choose a manager to lead their team. Again they should justify their reasons for selecting their chosen manager (e.g. shows positive body language that show they trust the players)

Review: Allow the player's time to discuss their answers and create their team. Have the group nominate a spokesperson who will feedback their group's answers to the team. Based on these answers ask the players, as a team, to select one of the behaviours from the groups communication role-models to copy and show during the upcoming training session. For example, the group may decide they want to be positive and supportive of each other during the training session. Their challenge therefore in the session is to unconditionally show that positive and supportive behaviour throughout the entire session. Afterwards review with the team how well they think they were at displaying their communication skills.

68

King of the Road

To Add and Emphasise Communication

P romote

Group Work: To increase and encourage communication between players, pair up the players in each team and give each team 6 footballs. The blue guards are now free to move from their gates and work as a pair to defend the gates. The red and yellow players now move out into the middle with a football and play against the blue guards 2v2, trying to score in one of the four gates on their side of the grid.

R ole model

O wnership

Communication Triggers: To emphasise the players ability to 'help' each other more effectively, develop communication triggers between defending players by adding a football to the practice. For example, the defensive players could develop actions from the triggers "Press", "Show Inside", or "Drop". Similarly the attacking players may communicate for the pass verbally by stating which foot they wish to receive the ball ("Yes John, right foot!").

G row

To Reinforce Commitment

R einforce

E mpower
support

Choose one of the methods for this practice targeted at emphasising commitment.

Example: Sweat 'o' Meter: Stop the practice and use the idea of a sweat 'o' meter to gauge the efforts of the players.

S upport
supporter

S elf-review

Practice Set Up

- Set up a pitch of an appropriate size for the number and age of the players
- Arrange eight 'mini gates' as shown in the diagram above
- Organise three teams of four players: four blue guards and two teams of four attackers
- The four blue 'guards' defend two of the mini gates each
- The red and yellow players stand on each side of the grid with four cones
- The red players attack the top blue guards, and the yellow players attack the bottom two blue guards

Practice Organisation

- When the coach shouts "Go!" the first red and yellow players pick up a cone and choose which of their two goals to attack
- The aim is for the red and yellow players to get past the blue guard, run through one of the two gates and put their cone down behind the gate
- If the red and yellow players achieve this they score 1 point for their team
- The blue guards get a point each time they 'tag' the attacking player
- At that point the attacking player drops their cone and joins the back of their line
- Each player takes it in turns to attack the guards and the winner is the team with the most points (cones through the gates) at the end of four attacks

Warm Up Exercise

P romote

R ole model

O wnership

G row

R einforce

E mpower support

S upport supporter

S elf-review

To Add and Emphasise Communication

Oscar Winning Communication: The coach 'role models' excellent examples of communication. During the practice offer the players your Oscar winning performance for 'Best Communication' in a Leading Role and highlight the key points from your performance. Award a 'Best Communicator' award to a player, or players, at the end of the practice or training session. If using this strategy with older players, you may wish to extend the 'Best Communicator' award to a Supporting Role. Offer the players your example of the best supporting role for teammates.

HELPA check-up: To monitor levels of communication amongst the team, the coach can ask players for a 'HELPA check-up' whereby the coach quickly runs through each letter and players offer a view of how each communication element is performing within the team. What can you improve on? Can you end the practice strongly? For younger players you may wish to specifically focus in on the 'helping' and 'listening' aspects. For older players, each part of 'HELPA' should be given equal weight.

To Reinforce Commitment

Choose one of the methods for this practice targeted at 'adding in' commitment.

Example: Which Pitch? What pitch are you ready to train on today? If a player believes they are showing a level of effort worthy of being in a 'higher league', they can request a 'transfer'.

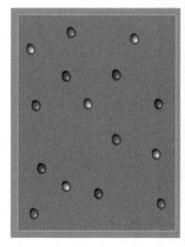

Practice Set Up

- Set up a practice area of 25 yards x 25 yards for three teams of five players as shown above
- The size of the area can be amended as necessary according to the age and ability of the players in the group
- To begin the practice ask the players to move freely around the area

Practice Organisation

- One team is designated as the 'trigger' group and is given a 'trigger' movement (for example: hopping, skipping, side-stepping, running backwards)
- The other two teams are given a movement to perform in response to the trigger group
- At any time a nominated player in the 'trigger' group can 'trigger' the activity by performing their movement
- For example, the trigger group runs fast weaving in and out of the other two groups, while the remaining groups balance on one leg.
- The coach changes the activities for each group and changes the 'trigger' practice

Pass and Move

Warm Up Exercise

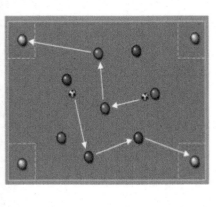

To Add and Emphasise Communication

P romote

Communication Triggers: To emphasise the player's ability to 'help' each other more effectively condition the players to communicate for the pass verbally and non-verbally. The players can point where they wish to receive the pass, or use a communication trigger that indicates that a player within the group (other than the passer) has to switch places with a player in the target box, to encourage off the ball communication between the players.

R ole model

O wnership

Opposed Practice: Adjust the makeup of the teams to add opposition to the team in possession to encourage them to provide information regarding time on the ball and their support positions. For example, one player from each team becomes a defender to play 3v1, or have the red and blue team oppose each other 4v4 and play with only two yellow target players. The other yellow players become neutral players in the grid to create 6v4 for the team in possession.

G row

R einforce

Team Captain: Allow only one player per group to communicate for a designated period of time. That player leads the team's communication for others to follow his instructions, and provides feedback to his teammates on ways to improve performance, including praise and

To Reinforce Commitment

E mpower
   support

Choose one of the methods targeted at 'adding in' commitment.

S upport
   supporter

S elf-review

Example: Stepping it Up: Challenge the players to move the ball between the target players in different ways.

Practice Set Up

- Organise a pitch of 25 yards x 15 yards
- Set up four small 'target' boxes in the corners of the pitch
- Split the group into three teams of four
- One group of four is positioned in the target boxes (yellow)
- The remaining groups of four (red and blue) spread themselves out in the middle of the grid
- Each of the middle groups have a football each

Practice Organisation

- The middle red and blue teams look to pass the ball between them
- The aim is to pass the ball into a yellow target player in each corner until they have passed the ball to all four corners
- Each player must touch the ball before it is played into a corner
- The teams can pass into the corners in any order they wish
- Both groups are aiming to do this faster than the other group

71

Chapter 4

P romote	
R ole model	
O wnership	
G row	
R einforce	
E mpower support	
S upport supporter	
S elf-review	

To Add and Emphasise Communication

Group Work: To increase and encourage communication between players add one football per team. The player in possession of the ball cannot be tagged. The attacking players now must communicate as a team to move the ball quickly to avoid a teammate being 'tagged'.

Better HELPA: When a player perceives the need for better communication due to a lack of help/support or poor/negative quality communication that doesn't help performance in their role, they can request 'better HELPA' from their teammates. It is important for a coach to role play a few examples first so that players see this process as normal and critical if the team is to do its job appropriately for each team member. This will help to build leadership and respect in teams, whilst demonstrating to teammates that players may have very different individual needs in terms of preferred communication styles.

To Reinforce Commitment

Choose one of the methods targeted at 'emphasising' commitment.

Example: Player Ownership: Change the exercises in the boxes to allow the players to choose a skill or activity they feel they wish to work on, or improve.

Practice Set Up

- Set up an area of 25 yards x 25 yards is organised with four corner boxes marked as shown in the diagram
- Amend the size of the area as necessary according to the age and ability of the players in the group
- Organise three teams of four players, with one team designated as the 'tagging' team (in the diagram above the yellow team has been designated the 'tagging' team)
- The practice starts in the central area

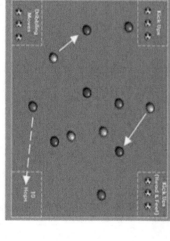

Practice Organisation

- The tagging team are given 60 seconds to try and tag as many players as possible
- If a player is tagged, they must go to one of the squares and perform the designated activity
- Once completed they can re-join the practice
- Swap the tagging team over after 60 seconds
- The challenge for the tagging team is to see if they can send every attacker to one of the activity squares in 60 seconds

72

Passing and Support Play

Main Session Exercise

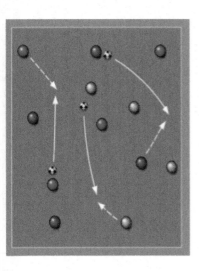

To Add and Emphasise Communication

Communication Triggers: To emphasise the players ability to 'help' each other more effectively, condition the players to communicate for the every pass verbally by stating which foot they wish to receive the ball ("Yes John, right foot!"), and/or non-verbally by pointing where they wish to receive the pass. You may also wish to develop trigger words such as, "hold" or "turn" for the players to implementing order to help the player in possession of the ball.

Oscar Winning Communication: The coach 'role models' excellent examples of communication. During the practice offer the players your Oscar winning performance for 'Best Communication' in Leading or Supporting roles and highlight the key points from your performance. Award a 'Best Communicator' award to a player, or players, at the end of the practice or training session. If using this strategy with older players, you may wish to extend the 'Best Communicator' award to a Supporting Role. Offer the players your example of the best supporting role for teammates.

Practice Set Up

- Set up a playing area of 20 yards x 20 yards
- Amend the size of the area as necessary according to the age and ability of the players in the group
- Three teams of four players start the practice in the area
- Each team has a football

Practice Organisation

- Each team passes the ball to and receives from the same colour teammates
- Players are looking to pass and receive in and around the other teams
- The teams score points for: receiving a pass within 5 yards of space; receiving a pass that goes between two other players; receiving a pass having performed an overlap; receiving a pass having performed a '1-2'
- Progress so that the player receives a pass from his own colour and performs a '1-2' with a different colour

P romote

R ole model

O wnership

G row

R einforce

E mpower
support

S upport
supporter

S elf-review

Chapter 4

To Add and Emphasise Commitment

P romote	
R ole model	
O wnership	
G row	
R einforce	
E mpower support	
S upport supporter	
S elf-review	

Simon Says: Begin to introduce verbal communication to the practice. If the coach says "Simon says, Mark can talk" then Mark is allowed to communicate with his teammates, and everyone else must stay silent. If the coach says "Mark can talk" then the player is unable to talk. If a player communicates when they are not supposed to (for example, the coach has said "Mark can talk" and the player starts talking) then a freekick is awarded to the opposition. Rotate players who can communicate every 1-2 minutes on each team, so if the coach says "Simon says, Andrew can talk", then Mark – his teammate - must now stay silent.

HELPA check-up: To monitor levels of communication amongst the team, the coach can ask players for a 'HELPA check-up' whereby the coach quickly runs through each letter and players offer a view of how each communication element is performing within the team. What can you improve on? Can you end the practice strongly? For younger players you may wish to specifically focus in on the 'helping and listening' aspects. For older players, each part of 'HELPA' should be given equal weight.

Practice Set Up

- Set up an area of 25 yards x 25 yards, with three scoring circle positioned in the grid
- Amend the size of the area as necessary according to the age and ability of the players in the group
- Organise two teams to play four red players against four blue players
- Add two yellow target players operate between the three scoring circles

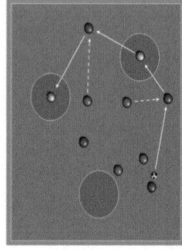

Practice Organisation

- Both teams compete for possession
- The target players are free to move between all of the scoring circles
- To score, one of the target players must receive a pass in a scoring circle
- If a goal is scored the ball returns to the attacking team and they look to score in a different circle
- The first team to score 10 points wins

74

Communication Focused Match

Main Session Exercise

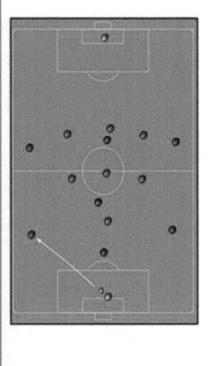

To Add and Emphasise Communication

Silent Soccer: Introduce a phase of the game where nobody is allowed to talk. Draw the player's attention to the other ways they communicate with their teammates through non-verbal means. For example, pointing to where they want a pass to go, applauding a teammate's intent, and the body language they present.

Silent vs. Vibrant Soccer: After a couple of minutes of the 'silent soccer' condition, allow one player per team to talk. Gradually increase the number of players who can talk per team until everyone is allowed to communicate. It is likely the pitch will be far more vibrant than at the start of the practice, therefore it is important to draw the player's attention to this. You may also wish to try playing one team that can communicate verbally against one team that must stay silent.

Communication Confidence Booster: To develop and help the player feel comfortable giving and receiving praise, build into the practice that the only communication allowed is praise or encouragement.

Practice Set Up

- Set up a playing area appropriate to number of players on each team and the age of the players
- Two equal teams each with a goalkeeper

Practice Organisation

- Play a normal game

P romote

R ole model

O wnership

G row

R einforce

E mpower
support

S upport
supporter

S elf-review

Chapter 4

P romote	
R ole model	
O wnership	
G row	
R einforce	
E mpower support	
S upport supporter	
S elf-review	

To Add and Emphasise Communication

World's Worst Communicator Ever: Ask your players to 'model' the worst communicator in the world. The players will 'overplay' the negative aspects (for example, total silence, harsh criticism at any small mistake, shouting personal remarks etc.), which magnifies these behaviours as very ineffective. Players will quickly realise that any behaviour like that really gets the team nowhere. Follow this up with your view of the teams' current communication levels and ask how they feel they can move further towards best communicators.

Team Captain: Allow only one player per group to communicate for a designated period of time. That player leads the team's communication for others to follow his instructions, and provides feedback to his teammates on ways to improve performance, including praise and encouragement. Gradually increase the number of players communicating until all players are free to talk.

Practice Set Up

- Use half a pitch with target gates marked on the halfway line and a goal at one end
- 13 players: 5 attacking players (blue), 4 defending players (red), 2 neutral players (yellow), a goalkeeper and a target player on the halfway line (green)
- The 2 neutral players play on the team in possession
- The practice starts by the coach playing into any of the attacking players (blue team)

Practice Organisation

- The attacking team, with the assistance of the 2 neutral players, attempt to break down the 4 defending players to score in the large goal
- If the defending team win possession of the ball they look to break-out and play through the target gates or to the target player
- The defending team scores a goal for reaching the target player as long as the pass is from the centre circle. A goal is also given for running the ball through either target gate
- The neutral players join the defending team when they are in possession

Divide and Conquer

Post Session Exercise

Foundation Phase and Youth Development Phase

P romote

R ole model

Session Purpose

- To 'close' the session down appropriately
- Work with the players to set a future direction for the next communication training session
- To collaborate with the player's to review the quality of team communication strategy use
- Provide the players with the opportunity to self-reflect on their own communication performance and judge what they have learnt from the training session

To Review Communication

O wnership

Allow the players the opportunity to review individual, group and team levels of communication from the training session.

Organisation: At the end of the training session ask the players to individually assess their own communication performance from the session. It may be useful to use the 'HELP A Check Up' strategy to guide the players' thoughts on what to evaluate. The players should identify one area (or part of the acronym) they performed well at, and why, as well as one area (or part of the acronym) they want to work on in the next session, and why.

G row

After allowing the individual players to consider their own performance ask the players to pair up. In their pairs the players share with their teammate their assessment of their own performance within the session and the reasons why. Next ask the pairs to pair up with another group. Within these new groups the original pairs explain to the new pairs what they learnt from their partner about their performance within the session and their reasons why. In this way you will be fostering a mutual exchange and supportive environment.

R einforce

Then ask the groups to pair up with another group to exchange each other's assessments of their own performances within the session and their areas for improvement. Finally ask these larger groups to feed back their session reviews to you. It is not necessary for you to hear every player's reflection on every teammate's performance, simply select a few different players from each of the larger groups. Draw the players to any similarities that may be developing and ask how, as a team, you can improve this in the next session. Similarly you may draw your player's attention to any differences that occur and use this as a means to highlight the fact that each player within the group has different communication needs which need to be respected.

E mpower support

S upport supporter

For players in the Youth Development Phase you may want to ask the players to pair up with the partner they had at the start of the previous debrief, at the start of the next training session. Task the partners with helping one another during the session to maintain their communication strength from the previous session, and help each other to work on the area they identified as an area to work on. For example, if one of the players identified that they wanted to improve their body language their partner can be an objective monitor of this, feeding back their observations during breaks in the session.

S elf-review

Chapter 4

Communication: Summary

Experience of watching youth football suggests to us that communication gets more and more important with age. We've witnessed tension and in-fighting within older youth teams because of position pressure and selection-deselection issues such that on-pitch communication is poor, or at worst, it shuts down. Without communication there is no team, merely a group of players on a pitch with individual self-interests.

Within an interactive team sport where coordination of resources and consistency of motivation depend so much on effective communication, it is a psychosocial priority for the youth coach to appraise, teach, and develop communication skills. In sum, we know that what players say (or do) to each other and how players receive such information can have a tremendous impact on performance (positive and negative), yet rarely do youth players devote any intentional and specific time to these skills. A coach's challenge is to introduce and develop communication as a valued skill right from the start.

Coaching strategies and behaviours summary

Strategy	Targeting Communication					Development Phase	
	Help	Encourage	Listen	Praise	Accept	5-11	12-16
Better HELPA	●	●	●	●	●	○	●
Communication Confidence Booster	○	●	●	●	●	○	●
Communication Triggers	●	○	●	○	○	●	●
Group Work	●	○	●	○	●	●	●
HELPA Check Up	●	●	●	●	●	●	●
Opposed Practice	●	●	●	○	●	●	●
Oscar Winning Communication	○	●	●	●	●	●	●
Silent Soccer	●	○	○	○	●	○	●
Silent vs. Vibrant Soccer	○	●	●	●	●	○	●
Simon Says	●	○	●	○	○	●	○
Team Captain	○	●	●	●	●	○	●
World's Worst Communication Ever	●	●	●	●	●	○	●

Key:

○   Not the focus of this strategy/not appropriate for this age group

●   Focus of this exercise/appropriate for this age group

5

Concentration

The third 'C' in the 5C framework is Concentration. Whilst high quality Commitment and Communication skills equip the player to make potentially significant performance contributions, it is Concentration and Control (the following 'C') which play key roles in **regulating** the quality of their performance. Concentration reflects a player's ability to sustain attention on an object, a person(s), a thought, a feeling, an action or goal for a defined period of time (e.g., 5, 10, 60 seconds; 10, 15, 30 minutes etc.). The quality of this concentration is determined by two factors:

- **attentional focus** (i.e., where their focus of attention is placed)
- **attention span** (i.e., the ability to remain focused and/or hold attention on certain objects, people, thoughts or feelings for a required length of time without being distracted).

Research has shown that expert players have superior knowledge structures to non-expert players. These top players know where to look, what to think, and what to say to themselves - relevant and positive to the task, or situation at hand. There are potentially 1,000 different activities that occur within any one football match, equivalent to a break in the level or type of activity once every 6 seconds. This requires elite players to have mastered making small visual fixations and 'chunking' perceived key information together, recognising its importance for their performance based on past experience, or the current state of the game. Together the players' ability to focus on and regulate these aspects is evidenced by the decisions they make and this reflects their ability to 'concentrate'.

One of most salient points related to concentration in youth soccer is the time spent by players **off the ball**, when not in possession, or involved in the immediate action. Attentional skills when involved in play, including the management of distractions and the training of peripheral vision, are important. Research consistently shows that top level footballers spend only 2% of a game (or less than 2 minutes) in personal possession of the ball. Whilst time in possession of the ball may not have been quantified in youth football to the same degree, it is relatively safe to assume that the vast majority of a youth player's game is spent without the ball. Effective concentration during this 'off the ball' time is illustrated by a player's anticipatory movements, their observation of opponents, read of the game, ability to lose markers, commitments to find space and make runs. Players deploying skilful 'attention' off the ball are smartly predicting the movements required to contribute to defensive or attacking roles in advance of the situation or scenario actually happening. Effective concentration in this context is therefore about action through anticipation and prediction. When dealing with developing your player's concentration, simply ask yourself *"How far along are my players in developing this mental process – on the ball and off the ball?"*

Players' attentional abilities will differ depending on their age and it is important for coaches to reflect on their expectations of players at different developmental stages. Therefore as with all the 'Cs' so far it is a highly useful exercise to consider the behaviours that you would expect to see in a player with excellent **concentration skills**. You can do this either as a solitary endeavour, or as part of a group discussion with your players. Consider what would be the key characteristics and behaviours that you would pick out of players with excellent concentration skills? What would you ideally expect of the age group that you are working with?

If you and your players reflect on these expectations carefully, you will now have a behavioural blueprint of what skills and behaviours you might like to promote within your coaching. You may also wish to consider what the opposite list might look like. The table below presents examples of key characteristics that differentiate players with excellent versus poor concentration skills, as reflected upon by coaches of senior players.

- Adopt the right positions in open play, showing good positional awareness
- Make a high percentage of correct decisions when releasing the ball
- Accurately pass at a high level and is very aware of the movements of teammates and use of space
- Track runners consistently and stay close to his man at all times
- Stay focused on their role at set pieces and corners, often organising others as well
- Respond quickly to the instructions of his teammates
- Win a high percentage of personal battles against similar standard opponents
- Refocus immediately on their role and position after a break in play
- Accurately recognises cues/triggers to act
- Anticipate opponents' movements and react more quickly to danger
- Communicate important information to others as they read the game
- Focus intently 'off the ball' when not involved in play, and create appropriate space and opportunities to be involved
- Stay appropriately focused on his role, even when tired/towards the end of the game

Fig 5.1.1: Characteristics of players with excellent levels of concentration

- Be easily distracted
- Fail to pick up man at set pieces due to lack of rehearsal/planning or communication
- Fail to refocus quickly after a mistake or break in play
- Drift out of position
- Dwell on mistakes and begins to play negatively
- Focus on actions that may make him feel better or gain sympathy
- Always be one step behind the pace/tempo of play
- Make poor decisions
- Contribute less off the ball to creating opportunities and space
- Fail to easily read opponents' movements and intentions when off the ball
- Fail to respond to teammates' instructions
- Fail to pick up on relevant cues/triggers to act on, or is slow in doing so
- Allow fatigue to impact on his ability to remain focused

Fig 5.1.2: Characteristics of players with poor levels of concentration

Concentration coaching: The fundamental knowledge required

What a player chooses to focus on, at any given time, impacts on the quality of subsequent decision making, feelings, thoughts and responses to an event. It will also affect their performance of a given skill, or skills. In terms of coaching concentration, the coach is essentially coaching 'attentional control'. This is because a player might have excellent concentration on completely the wrong object, person, thought, or event. Therefore, a player's focus of attention is key.

Younger players are developing their attention spans and may not be able to concentrate on the requirements of the task for long periods without switching off through mental fatigue, or focusing on material that is irrelevant to the task set. This, however, is unlikely to be the case in highly motivated players within your sessions and if drills and exercises are highly stimulating. A more frequent challenge may be that the young player focuses on negative thoughts associated with failure at the task, and dwells on mistakes which divert their attentional resources from the demands of the drill. Alternatively, they may get bored of the drill, find it too easy, and focus on doing their own thing. In sum, there may be a number of distractions in the environment which cause them to divert their concentration, and therefore concentration training can involve creating distractions within which players need to stay focused on the targeted skill/object. The key here is that we want young players to hold their focus on thoughts, objects, jobs, events or people that are *directly relevant* **to their immediate performance.** Of course, related to points mentioned earlier, their immediate performance includes time involved in play and time 'off the ball' but still contributing.

Coaching concentration skills begins by raising player's attentional awareness and educating them on the different forms of attention that can be positive and negative to performance.

The four attentional channels

In the 1970's, an American sport psychologist called Robert Nideffer introduced coaches to a simple grid to explain where attention could be placed. As a teaching aid to players over 12 years old, and for your coaching sessions, it can be useful in helping to coach concentration and to educate players around the basic principles.

Using the grid below, take a look at the positive or relevant content that players may focus on in relation to the four basic channels.

External Focus

Narrow-External	Broad-External
What will my players be focusing on? • The ball • A teammate • An opponent • Focusing on a target/accuracy	**What will my players be focusing on?** • Teammate in open play • Identifying open space to move into • Opposition positioning • Awareness of the 'bigger picture'
Role in Performance: **Performing**	Role in Performance: **Scanning**
Narrow-Internal	Broad-Internal
What will my players be focusing on? An internal thought, image or feeling such as: • Feeling of contact of ball on boot • Positive thought/self-talk or attitude after an event (good/bad pass etc.) • Trigger word or image before an event (kicking, heading etc.)	**What will my players be focusing on?** • Thinking through strategy • Planning where to pass when given multiple options • Organising teammates and planning having sensed opportunities or problems on reading the game
Role in Performance: **Responding/Preparing**	Role in Performance: **Decision Making**

Narrow Focus · Broad Focus

Internal Focus

Fig 5.2: A football-specific example of Nideffer's four attentional channels grid to help teach concentration

For the sake of simplicity, players can switch very quickly from one channel to another in a training or match situation due to the continuous, intermittent and dynamic features of football. It would be fair to assume that all channels are accessed and processed to a greater or lesser extent during a match.

As noted, the above diagram paints the positive picture of attention when it is relevant and switching effectively between channels. Of course, there is the less positive and irrelevant side: players can focus externally on the wrong people (e.g., the referee and their decisions, a hostile opponent; negative comments from the touchline/crowd/coach); internally on negative thoughts, self-talk and feelings (e.g., fear of making another mistake; anger/hurt at a teammate's comment; anger at a teammate's mistake or their own error), and also broad-internally on matters nothing to do with the session or match (e.g., parents, schoolwork issues, exams, personal problems).

Concentration coaching aims to educate players about their foci of attention and train these foci so that performance is consistently optimised and not disrupted by negative or task-irrelevant distractions.

Concentration coaching: Developing optimally focused players

Concentration is a mental skill that players would often learn about from sport psychologists or from studying sport science as teenagers. However, it carries much more value coming from the coach, and its principles can be introduced at a much younger age than any exposure to a sport psychologist or book. Moreover, it is something that can be introduced, trained, and reinforced on the pitch by coaches who give the topic of concentration some intentional 'discussion' and practice time.

Young players need to understand that when they play football, it challenges them to give two types of effort: **physical effort** and **mental effort**. Further, that 'mental effort' is all about what the **eyes are doing** and what the **mind is thinking** to help them with their 'physical effort'. Young players from nine years upwards should be able to grasp these basic ideas from the coach and, from 11-12 years old, understand their 'attentional' channels (i.e., like TV channels; BBC, ITV, Sky Sports, Channel 4). Given this head start, they are much more likely to regulate their attention on their own. In its simplest form, your role is to intentionally value concentration and work through the basic principles!

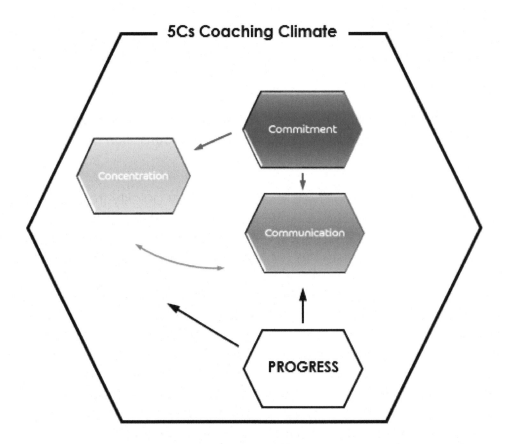

Fig 5.3: A climate that fosters concentration on the right things at the right time, allows a player to give maximal 'mental effort', as well as maximal 'physical effort', and be able to communicate accurate information and analyse situations effectively

Concentration: Coaching practices

Commitment to practicing and rehearsing the ability to focus and sustain focus on the right jobs, people, and responses in training, will help a player to maximise the robustness of their concentration. In the following section we present some strategies and behaviours within the 5C philosophy that allow your players to regularly practice their concentration skills so that they can stand up to the rigours of match play.

These strategies and behaviours aim to guide the coach towards what feels right and manageable for them. Some of these points will grab your attention and stimulate you more than others. Our advice is that you attempt to integrate these principles of concentration into your coaching sessions, supported by your intentional 'PROGRESS' of concentration with your players, particularly when you are using drills or games that are semi-open or open and require attentional switching. Other coaching behaviours and strategies may be reactive or spontaneous according to what has happened in the session, drawing from your ever-increasing 'tool box' of 5C skills and strategies, and specific to the age group that you are working with.

Practicing concentration skills means directing players to achieving specific attentional goals off the ball and when out of possession as much as time spent on the ball.

As a coach of younger players, it is important that you begin to challenge and develop their attention spans in small and large sided games. Small sided games and exercises offer children plenty of stimuli and involvement, testing their ability to react and process information quickly. However, you also need to challenge their attention with an 'off the ball' curriculum whereby they have to self-stimulate and be proactive with their attentional resources. In simple terms, the coach needs to *promote* the importance of positional responsibilities when 'off the ball' and make it engaging for young players.

It is important that young players see the attentional value and significance to being out of possession, as opposed to switching off. Setting appropriate challenges and goals for players when on and off the ball is therefore vital, as is challenging their mental effort towards the end of sessions to **stretch them** as tiredness and fatigue sets in. Catching players engaged in directing their attentional resources 'off the ball', *reinforcing* this, and encouraging teammates to catch each other focusing off the ball (with you '*supporting* *the support'*) will further highlight the value you place on this skill and strengthen its development in your players.

Each of the warm-up practices have been organised to allow you to retain some element of your communication coaching within the warm-up whilst adding in more robust concentration strategies as outlined in the practices. In doing so, you will be building a more rounded 5C climate. However, it is important that this doesn't detract from developing your player's concentration skills. Therefore this is, once more, left up to the coach to decide whether they wish to build communication elements into their concentration coaching as a further reminder and reinforcement, or focus solely on building their players' concentration skills. At the end of the chapter, we summarise the concentration strategies and behaviours used within the practices and give you an idea of what we think is best suited for younger and older players.

Concentration
Coaching practices

Practice	Part of the Session				Development Phase	
	Pre Session	Warm Up	Main Session	Post Session	5-11	12-16
Attention to Detail	●	●	●	●	●	●
King of the Road	●	●	●	●	●	●
Trigger	●	●	●	●	●	●
Pass and Move	●	●	●	●	●	●
Tag Game with Corner Boxes	●	●	●	●	●	●
Accurate Passing	●	●	●	●	●	●
Switching Pitches Small Sided Game	●	●	●	●	●	●
Trigger Word Small Sided Game	●	●	●	●	●	●
Support Play Possession Practice	●	●	●	●	●	●
What Went Well?	●	●	●	●	●	●

Key:

● Does not relate to this part of the session/not appropriate for this age group

● Relates to this part of the session/appropriate for this age group

P romote

R ole model

O wnership

G row

R einforce

E mpower

S upport
supporter

S elf-review

Session Purpose

- Draw the player's attention to the value and importance of concentration
- Begin to focus the player's thoughts on the upcoming session
- Give each player the opportunity to contribute through group discussions and allowing time for feedback
- Provide the chance for the players to interact with each other in a non-threatening environment
- Start to give the players ownership over their learning by allowing the players to lead discussions and the task

To Introduce Concentration

To develop the player's understanding of the important attentional cues specific to the unit and/or position they play.

Organisation: Draw the player's attention to the fact that the quality of their concentration is dependent on where they choose to place their attention at that moment in the game. They can have great concentration on an entirely the wrong players, areas of the pitch, events or thoughts. So if they practice focusing on the wrong things they will develop a negative habit that will prevent them from attending to what is really important in the game.

Split the players into groups based on their position (e.g. central defender) or unit (e.g. midfield) depending on the age of the players. Ask them as a group to consider the following questions. The first two questions are appropriate for the Foundation Phase, whilst the last three questions are appropriate to the Youth Development Phase. Again you may wish to tackle some of these questions over a number of sessions:

- What things do they think are important to focus on during training, or match, for their position?
- What things might potentially act as distractions to them in their positions that need to be avoided?
- Pick a situation (e.g. defending from crosses) and identify the key actions you need to focus on and who your key teammates are?
- What positive words/statements might you say to yourself during training, or match, to help you focus on the right things?
- What words/statements might you say to yourself, or to your teammates, to help regain your focus should you lose it during training, or match?

Review: Allow the players time to discuss their answers to these questions. Have the group nominate a spokesperson who will feedback their group's answers to the team. You may wish to probe the players further by asking them what the consequences might be to their performance by not focusing on the correct detail might have on their performance, and to the team. Challenge the players to focus their attention on the important detail related to their unit, or position, and use their positive words/statements appropriately for the entire session. At the end of the session review with the players how successful they were at focusing on the right detail and the right time.

Warm Up Exercise — Foundation Phase

To Add and Emphasise Concentration

P romote

Interference and Distraction: Pair up the players in each team and give each 6 footballs. Both the red and yellow groups attack at the same time. The pairs will act as

R ole model

distractions/interference to each other. The pairs can now attack any of the eight mini goals they wish, but only one team is allowed to attack a set of gates at any one time. The blue guards are free to move from their gates and work as a pair to defend the gates. The players now need to scan and assess where the space is to attack, where the defenders are to try and attack an unguarded goal, and plan their attacks.

O wnership

G row

Maintaining Focus: Stop the practice and ask the players how well they think they are concentrating on a scale 1 (not concentrating at all) to 10 (maximum concentration). Ask why do they think that and what can they do to raise their level of concentration a little higher for the rest of the practice (e.g., Do you think you can move from an 8 to a 9 in the next 5 minutes?).

R einforce

To Reinforce Communication

E mpower support

Choose one of the methods for this practice targeted at 'emphasising' communication.

S upport supporter

Example: Communication Triggers: Introduce a football to the practice. Condition the players to communicate for the pass verbally by stating which foot they wish to receive the ball ("Yes John, right foot!"), or by developing defensive communication triggers (e.g. "Press", or "Drop").

S elf-review
•

Practice Set Up

- Set up a pitch of an appropriate size for the number and age of the players
- Arrange eight 'mini gates' as shown in the diagram above
- Organise three teams of four players: four blue guards and two teams of four attackers
- The four blue 'guards' defend two of the mini gates each
- The red and yellow players stand on each side of the grid with four cones
- The red players attack the top blue guards, and the yellow players attack the bottom two blue guards

Practice Organisation

- When the coach shouts "Go!" the first red and yellow players pick up a cone and choose which of their two goals to attack
- The aim is for the red and yellow players to get past the blue guard, run through one of the two gates and put their cone down behind the gate
- If the red and yellow players achieve this they score 1 point for their team
- The blue guards get a point each time they 'tag' the attacking player
- At that point the attacking player drops their cone and joins the back of their line
- Each player takes it in turns to attack the guards and the winner is the team with the most points (cones through the gates) at the end of four attacks

Chapter 5

P romote

R ole model

O wnership

G row

R einforce

E mpower support

S upport supporter

S elf-review

To Add and Emphasise Concentration

Which Pitch? In a similar manner to the strategy in the Commitment chapter, draw the player's attention to the value of concentration. Pitch 1 is for those ready to train with Premiership levels of concentration. Pitch 2 etc. What pitch are you ready to train on today?

Oscar Winning Concentration: The coach excellent 'role model' examples of concentration to the players. During the practice offer the players your Oscar winning performance for 'Best Concentration' and highlight the key points from your performance, covering each of the attentional channels. Award a 'Most Focused' award to a player, or players, at the end of the practice or training session.

To Reinforce Communication

Choose one of the methods for this practice targeted at 'emphasising' communication.

Example: HELPA check-up: To monitor levels of communication amongst the team, the coach can ask players for a 'HELPA check-up' whereby the coach quickly runs through each letter and players offer a view of how each communication element is performing within the team.

Practice Set Up

- Set up a practice area of 25 yards x 25 yards for three teams of five players as shown above
- The size of the area can be amended as necessary according to the age and ability of the players in the group
- To begin the practice ask the players to move freely around the area

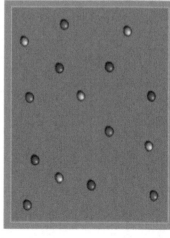

Practice Organisation

- One team is designated as the 'trigger' group and is given a 'trigger' movement (for example: hopping, skipping, side-stepping, running backwards)
- The other two teams are given a movement to perform in response to the trigger group
- At any time a nominated player in the 'trigger' group can 'trigger' the activity by performing their movement
- For example, the trigger group runs fast weaving in and out of the other two groups, while the remaining groups balance on one leg.
- The coach changes the activities for each group and changes the 'trigger' practice

Pass and Move

Warm Up Exercise · Youth Development Phase

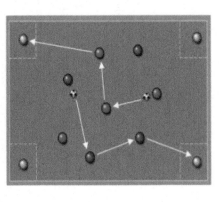

To Add and Emphasise Concentration

Sharpen the Senses: To heighten your player's sensory awareness, ask the players to focus solely on the ball as it arrives and leaves their foot tracking it to their teammate. Then, in turn; ask the player to focus on their footwork when receiving the pass; ask the player to switch their attention to their breathing as they receive and release the ball; ask the players to focus on the feel of their boot making contact with the ball to execute a perfectly weighted and accurate pass; ask the players to switch their attention to the sound of their boot making perfect contact with the ball, for that perfect pass; ask the players add a trigger word (e.g. firm) to use on contact with the ball.

Setting a Goal: To look to extend the player's attention at the point at which you feel their focus is wandering, set the teams a goal to achieve in the remaining time of the practice. For example, can they make 5 consecutive passes? If they do so, their team will gain an extra bonus point. This can also be used with individual players whose focus wanders towards the end of practices by setting them individual targets to achieve. For example, can they make 3 forward runs beyond the ball in the time remaining? After the exercise it is important to review with the players the importance of maintaining and renewing their concentration levels.

To Reinforce Communication

Choose one of the methods targeted at 'adding in' communication.

Example: Team Captain: Allow one player per group to communicate for a designated period of time. That player leads the team's communication for others to. Gradually increase the number of players communicating until all players

Practice Set Up

- Organise a pitch of 25 yards x 15 yards
- Set up four small 'target' boxes in the corners of the pitch
- Split the group into three teams of four
- One group of four is positioned in the target boxes (yellow)
- The remaining groups of four (red and blue) spread themselves out in the middle of the grid
- Each of the middle groups have a football each

Practice Organisation

- The middle red and blue teams look to pass the ball between them
- The aim is to pass the ball into a yellow target player in each corner until they have passed the ball to all four corners
- Each player must touch the ball before it is played into a corner
- The teams can pass into the corners in any order they wish
- Both groups are aiming to do this faster than the other group

P romote

R ole model

○ wnership

G row

R einforce

E mpower support

S upport supporter

S elf-review

93

Chapter 5

To Add and Emphasise Concentration

Interference and Distraction: Give the non-tagging players a ball each. The players now needs to be aware of where the open spaces are and where the tagging players are and plan ahead.

Switching Channels: Introduce the four attentional channels to the players and assign each one a TV channel. One player per team is designated the role of calling out a TV channel that relates to one of the attentional channels for their team. For example, if a player shouts:

- "BBC1" - Narrow External: Players have to focus entirely on one other person or the ball
- "Sky Sports" – Broad Internal: Players have to replay in their mind, for example, a skills/move to beat a player from their favourite player
- "ITV" – Broad External: All players have to scan the rest of team picking out the colour of a cone/bib the coach holds up, or different hair colours of the team
- "Channel 4" – Narrow Internal: All players have to think of a positive word that describes them as a player and repeat to

To Reinforce Communication

Choose one of the methods targeted at 'emphasising' communication.

Example: Better HELPA: During breaks in the practice allow the players the freedom to request 'better HELPA' and develop their leadership and initiative towards optimising communication preferences.

P romote

R ole model

O wnership

R einforce

G row

E mpower
support

S upport
supporter

S elf-review

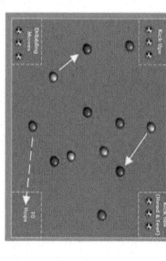

Practice Set Up

- Set up an area of 25 yards x 25 yards is organised with four corner boxes marked as shown in the diagram
- Amend the size of the area as necessary according to the age and ability of the players in the group
- Organise three teams of four players, with one team designated as the 'tagging' team (in the diagram above the yellow team has been designated the 'tagging' team)
- The practice starts in the central area

Practice Organisation

- The tagging team are given 60 seconds to try and tag as many players as possible
- If a player is tagged, they must go to one of the squares and perform the designated activity
- Once completed they can re-join the practice
- Swap the tagging team over after 60 seconds
- The challenge for the tagging team is to see if they can send every attacker to one of the activity squares in 60 seconds

94

Main Session Exercise

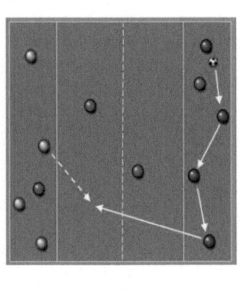

To Add and Emphasise Concentration

P romote

Most Distracted Player Ever: Ask your players to 'model' the most distracted and unfocused player ever. The players will 'overplay' the negative aspects (for example, looking at the sun; chatting to a teammate or someone in the crowd; talking to the ref while the game passes by; lying down for a rest after another mistake). Such a fun task 'with a message' magnifies these behaviours as irrelevant and damaging. Assist players in their learning of what their eyes and their mind should be focused on to optimise their contributions.

R ole model

O wnership

Silent Soccer: Run the practice without verbal communication to force the players to be constantly scanning the pitch and not rely on teammate's communication.

G row

R einforce

Maintaining Focus: Stop the practice towards the end of the practice and ask the players how well they think they are concentrating on a scale 1 (not concentrating at all) to 10 (maximum concentration). Can they look to raise their level of concentration for the final 10 minutes of the practice?

E mpower
support

S upport
supporter

S elf-review

Practice Set Up

- Set up an area of 25 yards x 20 yards, split into four equal zones
- Organise 12 players split into three teams of four players (red and yellow attackers, and blue defenders)
- The practice consists of 4v1 in the two end zones with one defender in each of the middle zones

Practice Organisation

- At each end of the pitch there are 4 attackers against 1 defender
- The aim is for the attacking team to create a chance to play a pass to the group at the other end
- A player from the receiving zone can drop into the central zone to receive, turn and pass into their group
- The defending players in the central zone can intercept the pass and mark/challenge the player dropping short
- Rotate the defending team so that each player has to the opportunity to press and also intercept
- After a designated time period, or number of attacks, change the defending team

95

Chapter 5

P romote	
R ole model	
O wnership	
G row	
R einforce	
E mpower support	
S upport supporter	
S elf-review	

To Add and Emphasise Communication

Concentration Triggers: Can the players recognise when to take advantage of the numerical advantage and start a counter attack? Can the players develop trigger words for when to initiate it? Similarly can the players recognise when they can go to pressurise the ball, or when they should drop and regroup? Can the players develop appropriate trigger words for this? Challenge players to develop their own personal trigger word to say to themselves, or perhaps a team trigger word.

Setting a Goal: To look to test and extend the player's attention when it begins to waver at the end of training sessions (e.g. in the last 10 minutes), by setting the teams (or individuals) a target, or goal, to achieve. For example, creating 3 attempts at goal from crosses. If they do so their team will receive a bonus point. Following the end of training session discuss with the players why it is important to maintain and renew their concentration in the closing stages of training and matches.

Practice Set Up

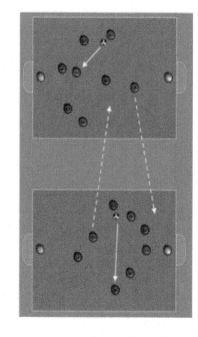

- Set up two pitches of approximately 40 yards x 25 yards side by side with a 5-7 yards gap in between each pitch
- Organise two teams of eight players split into four teams of four players with a goalkeeper in each of the goals
- Each player in the two red teams are numbered 1-4
- Each player in the blue team is numbered 5-8
- The goalkeepers remain in their goals at all times

Practice Organisation

- Play a normal game
- At random intervals the coach calls out a number from 1-4, or 5-8
- The two players with that number then must immediately leave the pitch they are on and quickly join the opposite pitch
- As the players change pitches the game on both pitches continue, leaving one team temporarily short of a player

96

Trigger Word Small Sided Game

Main Session Exercise   Youth Development Phase

To Add and Emphasise Communication

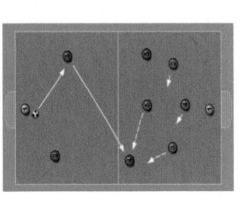

Concentration Triggers: Develop the use of the trigger words "Press" and "Drop" making sure the players use them at the appropriate moments.

Second Phases: To encourage your players to maintain their focus 'off the ball' introduce second phases to attacks. For example, if the ball rolls out of play, the coach immediately rolls another ball into the attacking team to recommence an attack on a different part of the pitch. Alternatively after a shot at goal, the coach can roll another ball into the penalty area to replicate a rebound for the attacking team. This can be extended so that it can be applied to the defensive team also for them to initiate counter attacks. Be sure to use this condition sparingly and with discretion so as to avoid the players always expecting a second ball, at the expense of promoting positive off the ball concentration.

Extra Time: To test and extend your players attention span split the game into two equal halves. In the first half the blue team start by pressing the red team high up the pitch when they lose the ball, and the red team defend deep in their own half when they lose the ball. Offside is in effect from the half way line. As a consequence the blue team should spend more time attacking in the first half to establish a lead. For the second half reverse roles so the odds are in favour of the red team attacking more frequently and forcing the blue team to defend (and hold onto their lead). For every goal the red team scores in the second half the time is extended by 3. For every goal the blue team scores in the second half time is reduced by 3 minutes, provided the second half is the same length as the first half. If the red team manage to score more than the blue team or draw the game, the red team win. The blue team can only win by scoring more than the red team. It may be advisable to start with a shorter duration for each half and then gradually increase the duration of the halves as the players concentration improves (e.g. start with 2x6 minutes, then increase to 2x7 minutes, 2x8 minutes etc).

Practice Set Up

- Set up a playing area of 40 yards x 25 yards with two goals at each end and a halfway line marked
- Amend the size of the area as necessary according to the age and ability of the players in the group
- Two teams of four players, each with a goalkeeper

Practice Organisation

- Play a normal match with one player per team designated as the team captain
- When a team loses possession of the ball, the team captain must decide whether the team is to defend in the attacking half, or drop and defend in the defending half
- If the team captain decides to defend in the attacking half, the team captain shouts "Press!" and the whole team must defend in the attacking half
- If the team captain decides to defend in the defensive half, the team captain shouts "Drop!" and the whole team must defend in the defending half
- Goals count double if the defending team occupy both halves of the

P romote

R ole model

O wnership

G row

R einforce

E mpower
   support

S upport
   supporter

S elf-review

Chapter 5

To Add and Emphasise Communication

P romote

R ole model

O wnership

G row

R einforce

E mpower
support

S upport
supporter

S elf-review

Commentator Football: The players are tasked with using only one word to signify where their attention is placed at that moment during the game, to trigger attention relevant to the immediate and upcoming performance. For example: "Ball – Press – Drop – Scan – Turn – Intercept". Each player's words will be very individual and specific to their positional roles. This strategy can be useful in forming powerful external and internal attentional habits. It will be helpful for the coach to role play this stream of dynamic attentional trigger words so that players can follow their lead and transition their attention seamlessly from one task/event to another.

Man to Man Marking: Play with two equal teams and pair the players up with a player from the opposition. Each player is now responsible for marking an opponent. Players 'off the ball now need to be able to switch their focus from where the ball is, where their man marker is and where the space is to receive and exploit. Players 'on the ball' now need to work harder to scan and find players who have escaped their marker.

Freeze Frame-Fast Forward: The coach stops the practice at random points and asks all the players to close their eyes. The coach then asks either an attacking player or a defending player to say where his teammates are positioned, where the opposition players are positioned and predict where the next pass might be played and why.

Practice Set Up

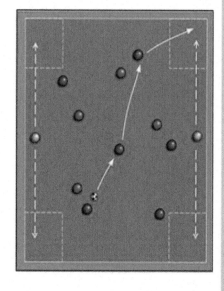

- Set up an area of 35 yards x 35 yards, with four scoring squares (one in each corner)
- Amend the size of the area as necessary according to the age and ability of the players in the group
- Two teams: One team of 6 players (red) and one team of 4 players (blue)
- Two yellow target players operate between two scoring squares each
- Rotate roles every few minutes

Practice Organisation

- Both teams compete for possession
- To score, one of the target players must receive a pass in a scoring square
- If a goal is scored the ball returns to the attacking team and they look to score in a different square
- After a designated period of time, replace the yellow target players with two red players. The two yellow players join the blue team, so now the blue team play 6v4 against the red team

Session Purpose

- To 'close' the session down appropriately
- Work with the players to set a future direction for the next concentration training session
- To collaborate with the player's to review the quality of team concentration strategy use
- Provide the players with the opportunity to self-reflect on their own concentration performance and judge what they have learnt from the training session

P romote

R ole model

To Review Concentration

Allow the players the opportunity to review individual and team concentration strategy use.

Organisation: Gather the players together after the session and ask the players to assess their own levels of concentration, and the wider teams ability to maintain its focus during the training session, by asking them to consider 'what went well...' and 'even better if... For example:

- *What went well*, in terms of our ability to concentrate as a team and individuals?
- *Our/your performance would be even better if* we improved on what aspects of our concentration?

It may be worthwhile noting down the players responses to these questions and reminding them of their answers at the start of the next session. The aspects of the players and teams concentration that 'went well' can be challenged to remain a strength, whilst the elements that could have been 'even better' can be the player's targets for the upcoming session.

O wnership

G row

R einforce

E mpower support

S upport supporter

S elf-review

99

Concentration: Summary

Many technical and tactical drills that football coaches know like the back of their hand will demand concentration skills. There will be drills and practices that you already do, similar to and better than the ones suggested here, that implicitly develop and challenge a player's attentional abilities. A host of your drills will target a player's information processing skills including their current perception and decision making capacities in the midst of interfering information. Other practices will challenge them to focus on thoughts, images, objects, intentions and reactions that test their ability to stay in the present (and anticipate their future!). Your concentration coaching climate is already shaping up.

The added value that we are asking of coaches to supercharge this climate is to educate players about concentration, and about where it can be located. Coaches, through their teaching practice, can introduce players to the different attentional cues that can direct and manage their technical, physical and tactical contributions. Coaches are skilled enough to guide players' mental efforts and help them to train where their eyes should be placed to process the action, and what their head should be saying to be part of the action!

Coaching strategies and behaviours summary

Strategy	Targeting Concentration				Development Phase	
	Narrow-Internal	Narrow-External	Broad-Internal	Broad-External	5-11	12-16
Commentator Football	●	●	●	●	●	●
Concentration Triggers	●	●	●	●	●	●
Extra Time	●	●	●	●	●	●
Freeze Frame-Fast Forward	●	●	●	●	●	●
Interference and Distractions	●	●	●	●	●	●
Maintaining Focus	●	●	●	●	●	●
Man-to-Man Marking	●	●	●	●	●	●
Most Distracted Player Ever	●	●	●	●	●	●
Oscar Winning Concentration	●	●	●	●	●	●
Second Phases	●	●	●	●	●	●
Setting a Goal	●	●	●	●	●	●
Sharpen the Senses	●	●	●	●	●	●
Silent Soccer	●	●	●	●	●	●
Switching Channels	●	●	●	●	●	●
Which Pitch	●	●	●	●	●	●

Key:

● Not the focus of this strategy/not appropriate for this age group

● Focus of this exercise/appropriate for this age group

6
Control

The fourth 'C' in the 5C framework is Control. It is closely allied with Concentration because the two skills, together, regulate the player's focus of attention, their thoughts, and emotions. These skills, in turn, manage the quality of the technical, tactical, and physical performance of the player. Football can be a physical, volatile, unpredictable and often unjust sport - characterised by gamesmanship, hostility, and inconsistent officiating. When a match is personally meaningful to players and the consequence of the result is important to the team, complex cocktails of motivation and drive can incite highly emotional responses when game events go for (and against) the team.

Positively-oriented emotions include joy, happiness, elation, excitement (and often relief) when individual and team goals are satisfied (e.g., scoring a goal, equalizing, making a string of successful contributions, winning the game, earning a penalty or the run of play). In contrast, players can experience negative emotions such as excessive anxiety/fear, anger, frustration, shame/embarrassment, dejection/despair and guilt when they fail to reach their own expectations (or those that others have of them), when teammates fail to reach the player's expectations, or when key decisions go against the team.

Take a few moments to think about the last situation you found yourself in that excited you.

Now compare those thoughts and feelings to the last situation that caused you apprehension or fear.

There could be a variety of thoughts and feelings that you might list. These might include: an elevated or racing heart rate, quicker more-shallow breathing, butterflies in your stomach, muscle tension or trembling, sweaty palms, confusion, uncertainty and cluttered thinking - with images and visions conjured that switch between the past and the proximal future.

Although many of these symptoms are allied with experiencing fear, you may recognise that a number of physical and mental changes happen when you are both worried and excited. Control is, therefore, as much about helping players to learn how to not get ahead of themselves, as it is about how to understand, accept, prevent or manage the less pleasant emotions they experience.

Managing performance 'nerves', 'worry' and 'anticipatory excitement' is a fundamental and learned psychological skill. It is actually a psycho-physiological skill because the player is responsible for regulating their physical state (breathing, muscle tension, muscular control, heart rate) and the clarity of their mental state. The ability to control and manage one's emotions and thoughts is one of the most visible and tangible elements that we can see on a football pitch. Repeated examples of costly emotional responses and incompetent coping at the highest levels reinforce - to all coaches and players - that it is an important skill to master. It is often a skill that players realise they need yet, lamentably, start to train far too late into their development. Many young players do not train this skill at all to any intentional or purposeful level. Players tend to reach a certain standard of competitive football that coincides with experiencing greater stress and more intensive emotional demands, yet realise they've not mastered their emotions, their self-talk, or coping skills in preparation for these newer challenges and higher standards.

Coaches play a key role in helping young players to learn about self-control as such skills become vital the more a player transitions to higher levels.

Considering the qualities regarding self-control, what would you, or your players, identify as being the qualities of players who show excellent self-control? What would be the key characteristics and behaviours that you would pick out? What responses would you ideally expect of the age group that you are working with? Similarly what would the opposite list look like for those players who demonstrate poor self-control?

Your expectations of players around their preparatory strategies, within-game behaviours, and reactions will certainly differ according to age group. However, if you take a few minutes to reflect on your expectations, you will have a clearer blueprint of what you would like to promote within your coaching that you might have targeted less before. When we look at role model players within the senior game, here are the behaviours that a group of coaches identified, contrasted against poorly controlled players. For youth coaches, there are plenty of positive behaviours to help young players master.

A player with excellent control will...

- Get up immediately after a tackle/foul and re-enter the game
- Get up slowly after a foul if it gives the team time to control the game and break the opponent's rhythm
- Maintain positive body language after a mistake and look to get immediately involved
- Appeal briefly to the referee in an adult manner in the hope of a favourable decision next time
- Build and maintain a positive rapport with the referee (either verbally or non-verbally)
- Show respect to the referee and offer praise, particularly after a good decision is made
- Respond swiftly and positively after either winning or losing a personal battle with his opponent
- Exert influence on teammates to stay in control and achieve the above
- Control arousal levels and mentally prepare for maximum effectiveness at corners and set pieces
- Help the team to speed things up or slow things down according to the score, time, or run of play
- Raise the energy levels of the team when teammates are going flat
- Motivate teammates for key periods/phases of the game

Fig 6.1.1: Characteristics of players with excellent levels of control

A player with poor control will...

- Disagree with the referee in an emotive and personal manner
- Over-argue a point and lose seconds of play while being out of position
- Physically retaliate
- Show excessive anger to an opponent/referee or own teammate
- Tackle wildly with or without intent to injure
- Over-celebrate after a goal
- Be complacent and fail to renew effort after a goal
- Fail to respond to failure when the game still offers plenty of opportunities
- Show repeated despondency at mistakes (their own/others) or injustices to the point of withdrawing effort or wimping out
- Blame other players for mistakes for which they were partly responsible, either verbally or by negative gestures and body language towards them
- Play tentative passes that result in losing possession
- Make errors by being passive and appearing lethargic during play

Fig 6.1.2: Characteristics of players with poor levels of control

Control: The fundamental knowledge required

Concentration and self-control skills are highly related. A player attending to external objects/people relevant to the game is most probably channelling his mental and emotional energy effectively and/or staying composed. In contrast the attentional focus of less controlled players tends to linger and fixate on a specific event, past or future situation, only serving to feed the emotion in a negative spiral. More controlled players have learned how to focus and direct this energy productively when things aren't going their way. For these players, the quality of the next touch, winning the next header, drawing support from a teammate, making a powerful run and closing a player down or impacting the game in the next 30 seconds are the key ingredients to their excellence in self-management. Any negative event or incident can serve to trigger a positive, thoughtful, disciplined, assertive and, most importantly, learned response.

Specifically these players will have mastered their self-talk, body language and breathing - three features that can be inextricably linked. Self-talk is the often constant and automatic 'inner voice' we have that influences what we think, how we feel, and what we do. The great players have learnt how to create an internal environment where what they say to themselves drives them forwards with more energy to the next action. While negative internal dialogue may occur, skilled players are able to let this pass through, then reshape and reinterpret the situation in order to commit to clearer positive thinking. Whilst it is difficult for coaches to interpret what a player is saying to themselves, they can often use the player's body language as a guide; self-talk is often betrayed by body language. If you think back to the last match your team played and recall a decision that was given against your team and the reactions of your players, you will probably understand what we mean!

Effective coaching of a player's self-control starts by giving attention to their breathing, body language and self-talk – all key elements of emotional self-regulation.

The 'mental calmness' of the mind and body to allow the player to perform at their best is also a by-product of their breathing. When under pressure players' breathing can become shallower and faster, depriving the working muscles of much needed oxygen. When this happens, our muscles become tense, actions become tentative and performances become rigid and uncertain. Typically when a player is calm, or in control, their breathing is deep, smooth, and rhythmic. Performances become more tension-free, fluent, and automatic when a player is able to master this physical state.

Few players are taught how to breathe properly in order to control unwanted tension, help focus their attention, and enhance their performance. The simplest technique to actively use - and the basis for additional breathing strategies - is rhythmic breathing. In this form of breathing, the player is encouraged to breathe to a certain rhythm. For example, inhaling for a count of four seconds, holding for three seconds, and exhaling fully for four seconds.

It is the exhalation (the long breath out) that positively influences a sensation of relaxation and a state of composure.

This exercise would start out as an off-pitch strategy to help players to become more self-aware and notice how relaxed, calm, tension-free and clear minded they can become. This relaxation process can gradually reduce in duration from 15 minutes at home, to 5-10 minutes in the dressing room to one minute before training to a matter of seconds on the pitch by using one to three deep breaths to regroup. The more breath training that players have done, the quicker they will feel the effects of single, centering breaths helping them to re-capture the required mental and physical state on demand.

How a player perceives or appraises a 'game event' (e.g., a goal, missing a vital chance, the awarding of a free kick) is also of great importance to a player's resultant self-talk and body language. If the player perceives the 'game event' positively then their self-talk is likely to be positive, which will be reflected in positive body language. Conversely if a player perceives the 'game event' negatively then their self-talk is likely to be negative, which will be more than likely betrayed by their body language. A player's interpretation of these 'game events' is therefore key and not all objectively 'negative' events bring about negative responses. Players can learn how to interpret and reframe negative situations in ways that lead to functional, if not positive behaviour.

The origins of this learning stem from the beliefs that players can be taught to hold about the nature of football, and indeed human nature in general. There are a series of plausible truths about football matches and training sessions that any player would have great difficulty arguing against. For example, take a look at the statements that are posed below and how you would behave as a player if you believed in and lived by these statements:

- Effort - individual and collective - is ultimately responsible for one of the most powerful emotions in your life – the sense of achievement. So, never give up!
- Mistakes, however small or large, are inevitable. They happen.
- Your own teammates will make mistakes

- The opposing team will make mistakes
- The officials will make mistakes
- Mistakes that you, your teammates, or the officials make are not done on purpose or with wilful intent
- Decisions that go against you can serve to heighten your vigour and inject you with a sense of purpose. You **can** act upon this positively and immediately.
- Opportunities to perform, to improve, and to demonstrate competitiveness exist right up to the final whistle, or end of the session
- The job of a player is to keep asking difficult questions of their opponent; to consistently test them no matter what the score or stage of the game
- You can maintain being a confident, resilient 'obstacle' to an opponent without them knowing what your true thoughts and feelings are
- Opponents have a right to fight for victory right up to the final whistle… they have rights and so do you. Respect these rights.
- Any session or game allows you to challenge your skills. If you don't accept this gift, then the skill will never be taken to new limits of performance
- Making the correct, often brave, decision is the most important part of the skill learning and execution process, because without it you'd be performing entirely the wrong task for the situation
- When you scold a teammate for making an error that had the right decision and intention behind it, you risk being the teammate responsible for them never making the right decision and intention again
- Reinforce a teammate's or your own efforts, and you are both likely to keep making the same, consistent effort
- Winning a match is a matter of performing hundreds of 'winning behaviours' across the team, and all you can do is contribute to as many as you can. That's all you can do.

The above list of examples represents what could be considered as **'Rules of Engagement'** for players that matter if one decides to subject oneself to the demands of competitive football. They represent realistic, rational, empowering beliefs, philosophies and expectations that can help the player to manage game situations and bulldoze their way through training and matchplay.

The challenge for coaches is that many players are not naturally driven by these types of beliefs, and they are not easily accessed or appreciated without awareness-building and rational discussion. Players may love playing football without caring to work on developing a more intelligent layer of understanding what the game is really demanding of them. The nature of football can chew them up mentally and the sport doesn't offer passionate players any special exemptions. Instead, unfortunately, many young players learn how to hold unrealistic, perfectionistic, or self-limiting beliefs that lead to unhelpful, excessive and negative expectations of themselves and others on the pitch. When players believe, for example, that mistakes are disastrous for them and that new skills should only be tried in practice sessions, one can imagine the levels of fear and anxiety that a young player may feel when a coach innocently challenges them to perform some new skills or duties in an important match.

Improved self-control stems from coaching players about rational beliefs and expectations to carry onto the pitch.

Negative, ruminating thoughts often preoccupy players as part of an ongoing internal dialogue. Whether it is thoughts about themselves and the consequences of their performance, thoughts about teammates, the opposition, referee, coach and parents or spectators, the origins of these thoughts are the **beliefs and expectations** that have been formed by the player.

As a coach, you play a critical 'cognitive' role in helping young players to understand and develop a smart, game intelligent set of beliefs by which to train and compete. Once they have these Rules of Engagement down, and they practice, practice, practice these values, then you will begin to see players acting upon positive thoughts that they have initiated because a helpful and empowering belief lies behind it.

Control coaching: Developing the optimally composed player

When considering your potential influence on the self-control of a young player, your reach as a coach extends to the quality of their preparation and discussions with them about the value of pre-match routines. Pre-match thoughts and feelings are important to master given the uncertainty of competition and match outcome. Therefore, the ability of young players to set appropriate goals, rehearse their successful role, manage very normal nervousness or excitement, and warm-up positively is a reflection of the important steps taken by a coach who values mental and emotional preparation.

On the pitch, teaching and coaching self-control to young players demands attention to the physical and mental components that will influence composure, arousal levels, and a state of readiness. Beyond working on their beliefs, introducing players to breathing strategies - and particularly deep, centred breathing - will help them to keep their nerves or anger in check... if and only if, it is practiced. In addition, work on their competitive physical image and body language can also be productive in helping the player to command a consistent physical presence (particularly after mistakes).

Mentally speaking, highly controlled players are exceptional thinkers within the 'narrow-internal' attentional channel (see Chapter 5 on Concentration). Driven by rational and optimistic beliefs, they have learned how to find a positive perspective, command word, phrase or image when adversity challenges them, or when complacency threatens and they need to refocus and energise themselves. They can build and commit to the next opportunity,

111

seamlessly detaching themselves from the past event (e.g., Next effort; Move on, I'm better than that). If, as a coach, you challenged your players to come up with the 'most negative statement when 2-0 down', you'd probably receive a range of options very quickly from players eager to respond. What if it was 'Most positive statement when 2-0 down'? I'm not sure that the range of statements would be offered up quite as quickly or plentifully. The teaching point here is that we need to help young players to harness helpful beliefs and build up their mental library of positive and meaningful phrases for the varying situations in which they will find themselves.

Mental effort is a critical ingredient to all of the strategies and objectives presented above. Players who are committed, hungry to learn, and intent on self-mastery will have more effortful mental resources at their disposal than those who are not as highly motivated. The role of the coach is to help young players to smartly deploy their mental efforts towards coping strategies and control skills that will help them to manage the emotional demands of the game. When the coach values and targets the development of self-control skills within their learning environment, then a control climate is fostered.

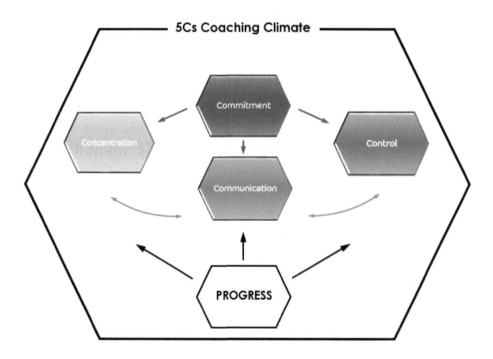

Fig 6.2: A climate that encourages self-control from all players will help players to regulate their thoughts, emotions and behaviour through having the correct focus of attention.

Control: Coaching practices

On the training pitch, players have the chance to practice working with their emotions. A common misconception is that emotional control is simply about reducing unwanted anxiety and tension in football. It is much more than this. It is about developing the ability to trigger certain positive emotions and feelings on demand when they are needed the most. This can often be a good place to begin with your players when introducing and *promoting* the importance of emotional control. Controlling your emotions is about regulating a player's level of arousal to the demands of the game. It can be as much about increasing levels of vigour and passion, as it can be about reducing them to an appropriate level of energy for the situation.

Understanding what is best individually for your players and being able to achieve that level requires practice. Over the following pages we present strategies and behaviours themed around improving your player's control skills 'on the pitch', as well as ways to *promote* control pre-session, and facilitating *self-review* after the session. Together these contribute to your growing 'tool box' of methods to be able work on players' 5Cs. We acknowledge that every coach is different and you may have your own unique way of encouraging and *reinforcing* the value of self-control in your coaching climate. Some of these points will grab your attention and stimulate you more than others. Our advice is that you attempt to integrate these principles of emotional control purposefully in your coaching sessions, and look to carefully 'PROGRESS' them throughout, particularly when you are using drills or games that are semi-open or open. Other coaching behaviours and strategies may be reactive or spontaneous according to what has happened in the session, and the age group that you are working with.

The warm-up practices have been structured with the primary aim being to begin to raise awareness of emotions and to develop positive control skills and behaviours with your players. The prior chapter's elements of the previous 'C', concentration, have been retained should you wish to build on and reinforce a wider 5C climate. This is left up to the coach to decide upon based on their understanding of their capabilities and current needs. The chapter concludes with a summary of the control strategies and behaviours used within the practices and gives you an idea of what we think are best suited for use with younger and older players.

Control
Coaching practices

Practice	Part of the Session				Development Phase	
	Pre Session	Warm Up	Main Session	Post Session	5-11	12-16
What's Best for Me?	●	○	○	○	●	●
King of the Road	○	●	○	○	●	○
Trigger	○	●	○	○	●	○
Pass and Move	○	●	○	○	●	●
Tag Game with Corner Boxes	○	●	○	○	○	●
Playing with Emotions Game	●	○	●	○	●	●
'Relaxation Zone' Game	○	○	●	○	●	○
Bad Refereeing Game	○	○	●	○	○	●
Courage Under Fire	○	●	●	○	○	●
Where were our Emotions Today?	○	○	●	●	●	●

Key:

○   Does not relate to this part of the session/not appropriate for this age group

●   Relates to this part of the session/appropriate for this age group

Pre Session Exercise	Youth Development Phase

Session Purpose

- Draw the player's attention to the value and importance of control
- Begin to focus the player's thoughts on the upcoming session
- Give each player the opportunity to contribute through group discussions and allowing time for feedback
- Provide the chance for the players to interact with each other in a non-threatening environment
- Start to give the players ownership over their learning by allowing the players to lead discussions and the task

P romote

R ole model

To Introduce Control

Give the players the opportunity to experiment with their emotions and the effects that different states have on their performance.

Organisation: Begin by telling your players that they can largely decide what emotions they want to feel by accessing thoughts, images and memories that have a significant emotional meaning to them. Even though it is widely accepted that a state of high positive energy is best, there will be times when they need to feel composed, calm, relaxed for certain situations, and times when they need to feel a degree of anger, aggression and injustice to get the best out of themselves. As long as they have personal control over these emotions and feelings, then they'll be able to find emotional states that function for every situation.

Ask the players to try 'activating' a variety of different emotions on the training pitch. This will give them the chance to experience and master them. Ask the players to experiment turning up for training one day with a goal of being massively energetic, confident and 'up for it'. They may wish to use methods such as, music, DVDs, cue words, positive memories that they know will help them create this state of mind. Encourage the players to record the effects that their state of mind has on how they feel about their performances and productivity over a series of training sessions.

Review: Ask the players to consider the following questions at each stage:

- How did the players feel with their chosen emotion?
- Was it the right state for them?
- Do they feel it altered the performances in training, or a match at all, and if so why?
- What affect did they think their chosen emotion had on their teammates?
- Can they think of ways that they and their teammates can help them stay in their ideal emotional state?

Working in small groups, allow the players time to discuss their experiences, based on these questions and have a select number of players feedback to the group. Try to come up with a plan that helps everyone get to and remain in their preferred emotional state.

O wnership

G row

R einforce

E mpower
support

S upport
supporter

S elf-review

To Add and Emphasise Control

Control Monitoring: To monitor the player's level of self-control, stop the practice and ask the players to rate themselves on how well and how quickly they are able to get over mistakes/error (being tagged). Use a scale of 1 (not very good, and/or quickly) to 10 (excellent and/or very quickly). Can the players focus on improving their score within a time frame set by the coach (e.g. next 5 minutes)?

Best Response Ever: Challenge the players to role model or act out the most positive response to a particular situation that you give them. Narrow down on what the correct behaviour would be in a given circumstance (for example, response to a mistake, or poor decision) and give the players the opportunity to practice this. You could also challenge players to mimic a positive feeling (e.g., readiness; confidence) within the game.

To Reinforce Concentration

Choose one of the methods for this practice targeted at 'emphasising' concentration.

Example: Interference and Distraction: Pair up the players in each team and give each 6 footballs. Both the red and yellow groups attack at the same time. The pairs will act as distractions/interference to each other. The pairs can now attack any of the eight mini goals they wish. Only one team is allowed to attack a set of gates at any one time. The blue guards are now free to move from their gates and work as a pair to defend the gates.

P	romote
R	ole model
O	wnership
G	row
R	einforce
E	mpower support
S	upport supporter
S	elf-review

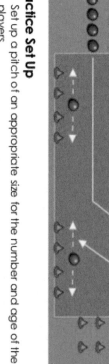

Practice Set Up

- Set up a pitch of an appropriate size for the number and age of the players
- Arrange eight 'mini gates' as shown in the diagram above
- Organise three teams of four players: four blue guards and two teams of four attackers
- The four blue 'guards' defend two of the mini gates each
- The red and yellow players stand on each side of the grid with four cones
- The red players attack the top blue guards, and the yellow players attack the bottom two blue guards

Practice Organisation

- When the coach shouts "Go!" the first red and yellow players pick up a cone and choose which of their two goals to attack
- The aim is for the red and yellow players to get past the blue guard, run through one of the two gates and put their cone down behind the gate
- If the red and yellow players achieve this they score 1 point for their team
- The blue guards get a point each time they 'tag' the attacking player
- At that point the attacking player drops their cone and joins the back of their line
- Each player takes it in turns to attack the guards and the winner is the team with the most points (cones through the gates) at the end of four attacks

Foundation Phase

Warm Up Exercise

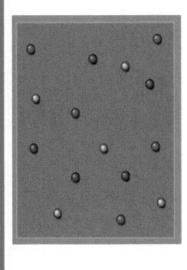

Practice Set Up

- Set up a practice area of 25 yards x 25 yards for three teams of five players as shown above
- The size of the area can be amended as necessary according to the age and ability of the players in the group
- To begin the practice ask the players to move freely around the area

Practice Organisation

- One team is designated as the 'trigger' group and is given a 'trigger' movement (for example: hopping, skipping, side-stepping, running backwards)
- The other two teams are given a movement to perform in response to the trigger group
- At any time a nominated player in the 'trigger' group can 'trigger' the activity by performing their movement
- For example, the trigger group runs fast weaving in and out of the other two groups, while the remaining groups balance on one leg.
- The coach changes the activities for each group and changes the 'trigger' practice

To Add and Emphasise Control

What is Control? To enhance the value in practicing different emotional control techniques, offer players who they feel have excellent self-control and composure. Many players will know what it feels like to be angry and nervous, so help them to identify why these emotions occur and how they can manage them. Many young players may not understand some of the emotions that they are feeling for the first time, and they'll tend to think that they are the only ones feeling this way. To realise that emotions are normal, experienced by all players, and that they are not alone can be a great relief to the young player. Your role is therefore to normalise that emotions happen, and help players to share and discuss the types of feelings that they can have, and how they can learn to master their feelings.

Which Pitch? In a similar manner to the strategy use in previous chapters, draw the player's attention to the value of control. Pitch 1 is for those ready to train with Premiership levels of emotional control, are energised, and 'up for' training. Pitch 4 is for those who are to train at League Two levels of emotional control, are flat, lethargic and 'not up for' training. What pitch are you ready to train on today?

To Reinforce Concentration

Choose one of the methods for this practice targeted at 'emphasising' concentration.

Example: Oscar Winning Concentration: The coach excellent 'role model' examples of concentration to the players. During the practice offer the players your Oscar winning performance for 'Best Concentration' and highlight the key points from your performance, covering each of the attentional channels.

P romote

R ole model

O wnership

G row

R einforce

E mpower support

S upport supporter

S elf-review

Chapter 6

Warm Up Exercise

To Add and Emphasise Control

Relaxation and Readying Zone: To foster mental calmness amongst the players, when a player passes into a target player they now switch places. The player entering the target zone uses this as a 'relaxation and readying zone'.

Breathing, Body Language and Self-talk: To develop a mental calmness in the players. Introduce and encourage players to focus on their breathing pattern, a positive physical presence of readiness and positive self-talk when outside of the practice as a target player, preparing to enter the practice when using the 'relaxation and readying zone'.

To Reinforce Concentration

Choose one of the methods targeted at 'adding in' concentration.

Example: Sharpen the Senses: To heighten your player's sensory awareness. Ask the players to focus their attention using each of the four attentional channels.

P romote	
R ole model	
O wnership	
G row	
R einforce	
E mpower support	
S upport supporter	
S elf-review	

Practice Set Up

- Organise a pitch of 25 yards x 15 yards
- Set up four small 'target' boxes in the corners of the pitch
- Split the group into three teams of four
- One group of four is positioned in the target boxes (yellow)
- The remaining groups of four (red and blue) spread themselves out in the middle of the grid
- Each of the middle groups have a football each

Practice Organisation

- The middle red and blue teams look to pass the ball between them
- The aim is to pass the ball into a yellow target player in each corner until they have passed the ball to all four corners
- Each player must touch the ball before it is played into a corner
- The teams can pass into the corners in any order they wish
- Both groups are aiming to do this faster than the other group

118

Tag Game with Corner Boxes

Warm Up Exercise | Youth Development Phase

To Add and Emphasise Control

Breathing, Body Language and Self-talk: To foster mental calmness in the players, introduce and practice controlled breathing patterns, positive body language and 'readying' self-talk (e.g., Swift and Sharp;) when in, and when leaving the corner areas.

Individual Rules of Engagement: To aid the player's coping and responding skills, allow the players to decide when they feel they have 'moved on' from the 'error/mistake' of being tagged. Before re-entering the players must give a sign to the coach, such as a 'thumbs up' or shout "I'm Back!" as an indication to the coach the player is ready to re-enter the practice.

To Reinforce Concentration

Choose one of the methods targeted at 'emphasising' concentration.

Example: Switching Channels: Introduce the four attentional channels to the players and assign each one a TV channel. One player on each team is designated the role of calling out a TV channel that relates to one of the attentional channels for their team.

Practice Set Up
- Set up an area of 25 yards x 25 yards is organised with four corner boxes marked as shown in the diagram
- Amend the size of the area as necessary according to the age and ability of the players in the group
- Organise three teams of four players, with one team designated as the 'tagging' team (in the diagram above the yellow team has been designated the 'tagging' team)
- The practice starts in the central area

Practice Organisation
- The tagging team are given 60 seconds to try and tag as many players as possible
- If a player is tagged, they must go to one of the squares and perform the designated activity
- Once completed they can re-join the practice
- Swap the tagging team over after 60 seconds
- The challenge for the tagging team is to see if they can send every attacker to one of the activity squares in 60 seconds

P romote
R ole model
O wnership
G row
R einforce
E mpower support
S upport supporter
S elf-review

119

Chapter 6

To Add and Emphasise Control

P romote

R ole model

O wnership

G row

R einforce

E mpower support

S upport supporter

S elf-review

Emotional Oscar Winners: To raise awareness around good emotional control, using 'role model' examples, and show the positive effects/consequences on each response on your game and performance. One team role models excellent examples of emotional control. During the game the players should show as many examples of composed, support, positive play, and be someone who can shrug off mistakes and move onto the next event.

World's Worst Response Ever: To raise awareness around poor emotional control, invite players to 'role model' examples and show the negative effects/consequences on each response on their game and performance. One team role models poor emotional control. During the game the players should act out being angry with teammates, show self-criticism, fear, despair or disinterest in the game.

Most Controlled Player Award: At the end of the practice, award a 'Most Controlled Player' award to the player (or players) who demonstrated the best control over their emotions. This can be a coach's award, or a player's player award decided by a player vote.

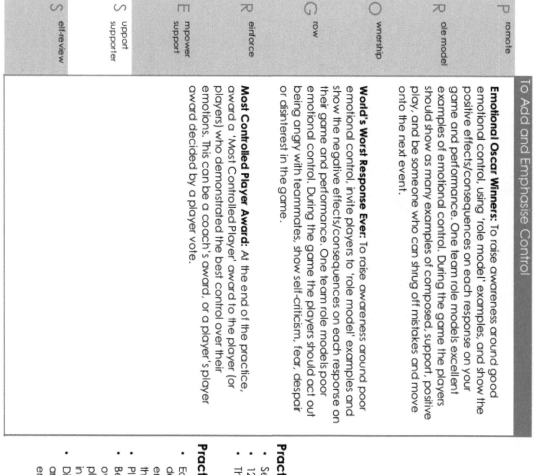

Practice Set Up

· Set up an area of 50 yards x 30 yards with goals at each end
· 12 players: two teams of 5v5 with one goalkeeper on each team
· The practice starts with a kick-off for one of the teams

Practice Organisation

· Each team is given a role to play during the game that focuses on demonstrating positive or negative emotions. In order to normalise emotions and feelings a good starting point is to 'act them out' so that the player has a clear 'awareness' of them
· Play for two equal periods and then switch roles at half-time
· Begin by giving the entire team the same emotional role to play, but over time you may wish to mix the teams up so each team consists of player's expressing different emotions, to explore the effect on individual and team performance
· Discuss with the players after the game the impact of their emotions and help them to realise the problems that can arise if they leave their emotions unchecked

'Relaxation Zone' Game

Main Session Exercise

To Add and Emphasise Control

Relaxation and Readying Zone: To improve the efficiency of the player's ability to get into a state of mental calmness, reduce the time players need to relax in the 'relaxation zone'.

Individual Rules of Engagement: To help the player's develop their coping and responding skills, ask the players to choose their own realistic triggers to momentarily compose and re-focus. Before re-engaging in the game, the players must give a sign to the coach, such as a 'thumbs up' or shout "I'm Back!" as an indication to the coach that the player is ready to re-enter the practice.

Control Monitoring: To monitor the player's level of self-control, the coach selects players at random during the practice and asks them to rate themselves on how well and how quickly they are able to re-compose and re-energise. Use a scale of 1 (not very good) to 10 (excellent). Can the player focus on improving their score within a time frame set by the coach (e.g. next 5 minutes)?

Practice Set Up

- Set up a playing area of 40 yards x 25 yards with 2 goals at each end
- Organise a small 'relaxation zone' to the side of the pitch
- Amend the size of the area as necessary according to the age and ability of the players in the group
- Arrange two teams of five players, each with a goalkeeper

Practice Organisation

- Play a normal match
- At random intervals during the game, the coach picks out one player from each team, who go to the 'relaxation zone' at the side of the pitch
- As play continues on the pitch, the two players use relaxation techniques to relax and re-focus. For example, focusing on breathing by taking deep breaths filling from the bottom of the stomach upwards to the top of the lungs, showing positive body language, and talking positively to themselves as they ready themselves to re-enter the game
- Start by asking the players to focus on this for 20 seconds before they re-enter the game and continue playing

P romote

R ole model

O wnership

G row

R einforce

E mpower support

S upport supporter

S elf-review

121

Chapter 6

Main Session Exercise

To Add and Emphasise Control

P romote	
R ole model	
G row	
O wnership	
R einforce	
E mpower support	
S upport supporter	
S elf-review	

Team Emotional Management Rules: To develop coping and responding skills, challenge each team to develop a team trigger word to cue players to stay composed and to stimulate a sense of readiness for the next action. For example, "No Lost Seconds" which, when called by a player, signifies the need for very quick responses and no arguing over mistakes or decisions.

Peer Error Management: Encourage teammates to detach a player from their mistake by offering immediate support. A teammate might say 'Next effort, Dan' or 'Back on it, Jack', such that the teammate is part of helping a player to manage their responses to mistakes.

Toughness Tests: To develop the player's range of emotional control skills under pressure, add match-related scenarios to the game. For example, add a referee who favours one team with his decisions, or overload one team by sending a player off, then continuing to give that team unfavourable decisions.

Relaxation and Readying Zone: If a player responds negatively to a referee decision, he is shown a 'relax and refocus' card and is sent to the 'relaxation zone' for 30 seconds. If he fails to practice 3 x deep breaths, composed body language, shouts 'Ready', he serves another 30 seconds.

Practice Set Up

- Set up a playing area of appropriate to number of players on each team and the age of the players
- Arrange two equal teams each with a goalkeeper
- One referee

Practice Organisation

- Play a normal game
- A referee officiates the game
- The referee periodically gives bad/wrong calls to simulate adversity and induce anger in players, thus allowing players to use their control strategies

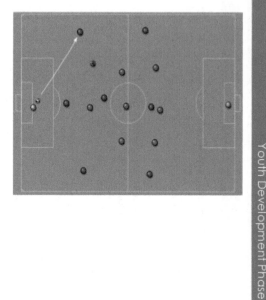

Courage Under Fire

Youth Development Phase

Main Session Exercise

To Add and Emphasise Control

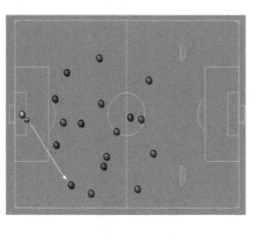

P romote

Toughness Tests: To test the player's range of emotional control skills under pressure, change the match-related scenario to the game. For example, increase the pressure on the red team by having them defend a 1-0 lead, or including poor refereeing decisions that favour the blue team.

R ole model

O wnership

Positive Football: Challenge the players to see how continuously they can communicate positive statements around the pitch and keep all players committed, focused, composed and confident regardless of events in the game. This is not an easy task to begin with as we typically don't practice speaking positively openly. You may wish to introduce a variation of this by rotating players every minute such that one player has the prime positive leadership responsibility. It will also be helpful for the coach to role play this first.

G row

R einforce

Emotional Confidence Booster: Whenever a set number of opposing players simultaneously see an opposition player respond negatively to a situation, they can shout "Confidence Booster". If the call is simultaneous they award themselves a freekick, possession of the ball, a penalty, or some reward agreed upon by both teams at the start of the game.

E mpower
support

S upport
supporter

S elf-review

Practice Set Up

- Use a full pitch, restricted in length with a normal goal at one end and two small goals across the width of the pitch
- Organise 19 players: 7 red players, 10 blue players and a goalkeeper arranged into a formation to suit your playing style
- The red team attack the two small goals
- The blue team attack the large goal
- Include normal offside

Practice Organisation

- Play a normal game
- The red team are 2-0 ahead
- Play for 10 minutes (i.e. the last 10 minutes of a game)
- The aim is for the red team to hold on to their lead despite having less players

Chapter 6

P romote

R ole model

O wnership

G row

R einforce

E mpower
support

S upport
supporter

S elf-review

Session Purpose
- To 'close' the session down appropriately
- Work with the players to set a future direction for the next control training session
- To collaborate with the player's to review the quality of team emotional control strategy use
- Provide the players with the opportunity to self-reflect on their own self-control performance and judge what they have learnt from the training session

To Review Control

Allow the players the opportunity to review individual and team control strategy use.

Organisation: Gather the players together after the session and ask the players to assess their own levels of emotional control, and the wider team's ability to maintain control during the training session, by using a simple traffic lights method. This is a quick and simple method of engaging the players regarding how to monitor their emotions on a regular basis. Ask the players whether they emotional control use was in the:

- Red - I/we were not very good at managing my/our emotions within the session, or were not appropriately 'activated' for the session
- Yellow - I/we were inconsistent at managing my/our emotions within the session, or were 'activated' for some of the practices but not all during the session
- Green - I/we were very good at managing my/our emotions within the session, and/or were appropriately 'activated' for the session

You may wish to record (or have the players record) the responses on a session basis for each player and the team. This will give you a graphical representation of the players and teams level of emotional control levels on a session by session basis. It may also be useful to display the scores for every player to see.

124

Control: Summary

Given that football can be a game that incites emotions, one of the main responsibilities of a youth coach is to help players to master their emotions so that they conserve and manage their energy effectively. Too often coaches and players leave self-control and stress management skills to chance, until players suddenly reach a level where they lack the coping skills to manage their own or others' inevitable indiscretions and mistakes. It can then be a frustrating journey onwards when all they needed to do was to spend time understanding their feelings (and the beliefs that trigger them) and practicing the optimal ways to behave as a player as they master new technical skills. These are values and behaviours that you can introduce and shape in youngsters from a pretty early age.

Coaching strategies and behaviours summary

Strategy		Targeting Control			Development Phase	
	Mental Calmness	Coping & Responding (Individual)	Coping & Responding (Peer)	Energising	5-11	12-16
Best Response Ever	•	•	•	•	•	•
Breathing, Body Language, Self-talk	•	•	•	•	•	•
Control Monitoring	•	•	•	•	•	•
Emotional Confidence Booster	•	•	•	•	•	•
Emotional Oscar Winners	•	•	•	•	•	•
Individual Rules of Engagement	•	•	•	•	•	•
Most Controlled Player Award	•	•	•	•	•	•

Strategy	Targeting Control				Development Phase	
	Mental Calmness	Coping & Responding (Individual)	Coping & Responding (Peer)	Energising	5-11	12-16
Peer Error Management	○	○	●	○	○	●
Positive Football	○	○	●	●	○	●
Relaxation and Readying Zone	●	○	○	●	●	●
Team Emotional Management Rules	○	●	●	○	○	●
Toughness Tests	●	●	●	●	○	●
What is Control?	●	●	●	●	●	●
Which Pitch?	●	●	●	●	●	●
World's Worst Response Ever	○	●	○	○	○	●

Key:

○ Not the focus of this strategy/not appropriate for this age group

● Focus of this exercise/appropriate for this age group

7
Confidence

As the final 'C', Confidence is positioned last in the 5C series primarily because it is developed, influenced, and united by the preceding four 'Cs'. As a clearly crucial factor to player development and performance, it is important for coaches to differentiate between confidence as a state of mind and confidence as a more enduring personal attribute.

In the context of a training session or a match, confidence is a psychological state empowered by the beliefs that a player has about executing specific skills to a desired level or achieving specific outcomes for themselves or the team. This state of mind can be affected by session or game events, and it is possible for beliefs to change and for confidence to fluctuate within matches and sessions on a moment-by-moment basis. Factors such as recent form, personal preparation, types of personal and team goals, the perception and style of the opposition, the form of teammates, the score and time remaining in a game can all elevate and diminish confidence. However, the most confident players seem to possess a shield of resilience that protects them from experiencing anything more than simply minor fluctuations in their mental approach to the task.

Therefore, the task for coaches is to envision confidence as a robust personal attribute that is resilient to situational events, and to help players to build it – brick by brick. Confidence can be developed and shaped much like Commitment, as an internal power built on a solid foundation of effort, skills, accomplishments, and support.

As with the other 'Cs' in this book, it is useful to consider what you notice in players when they possess high confidence compared to low confidence. What are the types of behaviours, specific to the age group that you coach, that you would expect to see in a confident player? What behaviours indicate a low level of confidence? This is a useful educational task to do with your players (typically from 11 years old onwards) so that you understand what their perceptions of confidence are, as well what they feel are their sources of confidence.

One of the most noticeable characteristics of confidence is its positive, forward-moving energy. As a force within the player, it rarely goes backwards on the pitch and only for strategic purposes! It allows the player to approach the challenges of the situation, as opposed to avoiding them, and it gives the player the power to take opportunities and make decisions that less-confident players might view as excessive risks or threats.

The table below details some of the characteristics of high and low confidence players offered by a number of age group coaches in the youth development phase

.

A player with excellent confidence will...

- Drive forward on or off the ball
- Involve themselves to receive the ball under pressure
- Demand the ball from teammates
- Be the player who wants the ball when the team are losing or under pressure
- Run to pick the ball up or get it back into play quickly and with a sense of urgency
- Maintain positive body language at all times to any event that occurs in a game
- Demonstrate inventive or creative play as opposed to making defensive decisions
- Maintain a spring in their step for 90 minutes
- Shoot when they see the option without fear of any negative evaluation or criticism if a mistake is made
- Attend to keeping other player's spirits high due to their own sense of security, competence and optimism

Fig 7.1.1: Characteristics of players with excellent levels of confidence

A player with poor confidence will...

- Let their head drop
- Exhibit poor body language
- Hide from the game, or be out of position and unavailable to pass to
- Not call for the ball
- Not want the ball
- Want to offload the ball quickly and often backwards
- Give up and not work as hard
- Look to blame others to divert attention away from themselves
- Play safe and avoid risks (even when risks are required) so as not to draw attention from any possible mistakes
- Be more easily irritable with other players due to a lesser sense of security and control
- Disengage from the game more readily, associated with feeling helpless or that all hope is lost

Fig 7.1.2: Characteristics of players with poor levels of confidence

Chapter 7

Confidence: The fundamental knowledge required

When considering your own thoughts and the table above, you'll notice that highly confident players possess features of commitment, communication, concentration and control. Indeed, although confidence is not a mental skill per se, it is built directly through the deliberate practice of developing the other four 'Cs'.

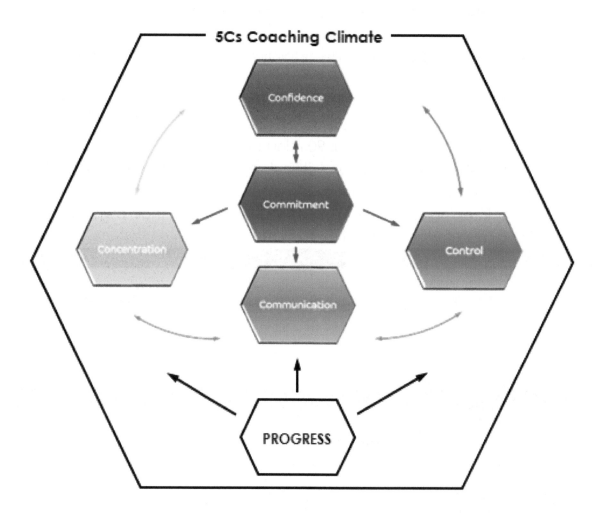

Fig 7.2: A climate aimed at developing enduring confidence in players will influence, and be built through the deliberate practice of the other 4Cs

It is important to reaffirm that being good at a skill is a key source of confidence. The phrase 'confidence comes from competence' is quite an accurate golden rule. However, it is what players do about maintaining this 'rule' that makes the difference. Some players might be highly competent technically or tactically but they fail to remind themselves regularly of the skills that they possess, the effort they have invested, and the accomplishments experienced because of those skills and investments. The coach functions as a bridge by reinforcing the links between effort and skilled achievements.

Coaches can help players to build their own robust confidence by ensuring that little successes, accomplishments and improvements are consistently acknowledged.

Imagine that skills are human beings for a moment and imagine a skill such as passing. How strong do you feel the belief or confidence of passing would become if it never received any feedback from a coach on its level of performance? Certainly not as strong as, say, tackling or heading who both received a great deal of praise and technical feedback on how good they were as well as being directed towards areas for improvement.

As a coach, it is important to understand the principles of confidence-building and how to manipulate and integrate these principles into your coaching sessions. Theoretically, the strongest source of confidence for players is **recent past accomplishments**. Therefore, picking out players' accomplishments or improvements, however small, serve as important reinforcement **feedback** to them. Remember that young players may not naturally do this themselves or 'big themselves up' so, whilst guarding against nurturing overconfident arrogance, it is beneficial for a coach to draw out examples of successes for players. In this respect, it is vital to attend specifically to what the player achieved, and to reinforce the effort that underpinned the achievement (i.e., strengthen the association between effort and skill execution).

The second strongest source of self-confidence for players is termed '**vicarious experience**', which emphasises how seeing someone else of a similar level, size, or background perform a skill successfully instils a sense of belief that the player can perform that skill too. For example, imagine if you decided to a do a bungee jump but had a sudden lack of confidence as you were transported to the top. A best friend of a similar height, inexperience, and craziness offers to go first and he succeeds in living! In doing this task first, he has role modelled the experience for you and you have lived the successful experience vicariously (i.e., through him) giving you the confidence that you'll also stay alive! In essence, "If he can do it, then so can I". Within soccer, the concept of vicarious experience doesn't quite work that simply, but the principle for coaches is to apply plenty of demonstrations and role modelling for players to give them a sense of possibilities. Often using elite player role models can work, and video footage of them demonstrating the skill is even better as it offers a clear visual reinforcement of the potential that is possible through hard work.

Confidence in players is positively influenced when coaches present personal, reachable possibilities to them, and credibly show them how.

Most importantly, coaches (and teammates) can consistently role model those (broader) skills that are important to player development and specific positional play. Following demonstrations, coaches should help the player set goals in training, or adopt a focus on improving the skill, so that the player experiences accomplishments – linking to the primary source of confidence. Finally, coaches should be on hand to encourage the player to review their accomplishments and efforts so that the player becomes more skilled at self-evaluating the broader qualities and skills that comprise their role as a player.

Building a player's competence stems from helping them to deposit accurate memories about how high the quality of that skill is becoming. A confident state of mind develops when the player's sub-conscious and conscious minds draw upon these memories. A confident player competes with their strengths at the forefront of their mind, and the coach's role is to help the player to programme these strengths, and keep them easily accessible for recall (e.g., "You have a massive engine, Lee, and it's because no one trains harder than you. Turn the key and put your foot down!")

As depicted above, one of the main ways that the coach can solidify self-confidence is to apply its next strongest source, technically termed **'verbal persuasion'**. This is when confidence is enhanced by someone valuable and important to the player telling them that they have what it takes, believing in their ability, and affirming their strengths. This is akin to positive self-talk, but it comes from a secondary source to the player. In football, the most important 'persuaders' of credible influence for young players are going to be the coach, fellow teammates, and parents... and most probably in that order depending on their age.

The 'I believe in you, you can do it' maxim goes a long way with young players, and the job of the coach is to create a confidence climate where players acknowledge and celebrate each other's strengths. This might be a new concept to some coaches who are used to working in a cultural environment where there is a poverty of recognising strengths. However, have faith that your positivity towards young players will help them to engage in more positive, strengths-based affirmations themselves. After all, vicariously they will start to copy you in affirming both themselves and other teammates. This can only be a good thing for a young player's self-esteem and communication skills. Players will start to cultivate a forward-moving approach, driven by positive beliefs, assisted by people who believe in their efforts.

There is a fourth source of self-confidence, linked to **emotional control**, which basically proposes that confident players are those that draw belief from knowing they have mastered their emotions and can find the right emotional state for the task. Of course, we have covered this knowledge under the Control 'C' and how the practice of breathing, body language, and self-talk helps to regulate our thoughts and feelings to confidently manage situations, positional roles, and tasks.

Confidence coaching: Developing players with optimal self-belief

Applying the knowledge above, confidence coaching revolves around managing three essential parameters within a session, each of which depends upon the other (i.e., interdependence).

1. Positive Attitude. You want to help players find and **maintain** a positive attitude and approach to learning in the session. This is a session in which positive body language and physical presence are encouraged; where players consistently think and talk in a positive manner in response to tests of skill and events in the session. It is a session where there is no fear of failure, only trying and learning, and where players bounce back physically and verbally from errors and trials almost as if bullets could bounce off them.

2. Positive Accomplishments. You want to ensure that there is plenty of opportunity for individual success, even small successes, by setting appropriate and progressive challenges/goals. The coach allows time for plenty of experience of success for perceived competence to develop before moving to the next level. In addition to new skills and challenges, the coach also allows players to focus on their **favourite drills** that give them the chance to showcase their **strengths** and maximise their opportunity to feel good about the elements at which they are strong.

3. Positive Support. You want to engage all players in the process of offering positive verbal support and praise to individual players when their efforts and attempts deserve reinforcement. Supporting a 'no fear of failure' climate means praising a player who has tried his personal best, even when the execution was not perfect but the intention was correct. This environment of positive support helps players 'want the ball more' even after a poor execution. In a non-supportive climate that creates a fear of mistakes, some players would hide or limit effort because their fragile confidence would cause them not to want to show greater incompetence.

When you create a cycle of **attitude** influencing **accomplishments** acknowledged by **support,** which in turn strengthens **attitude**, players are more likely to develop a 'shield' that protects them from experiencing any more than simply minor fluctuations in the power of their belief.

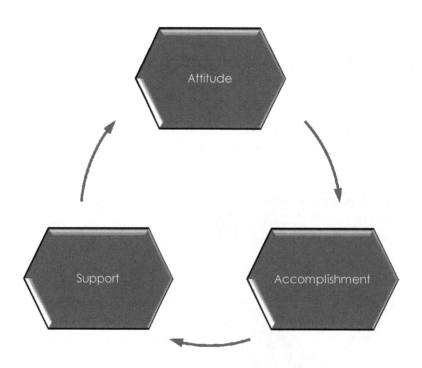

Fig 7.3: By encouraging a positive attitude, building accomplishments step-by-step, and offering positive support within the session, you will foster a more enduring level of confidence in your players.

Your coaching session therefore needs to tune into developing a learning environment where these three positives are experienced by players. A number of coaching practices and strategies will therefore target ways of integrating these three areas.

Confidence: Coaching practices

Whilst Confidence can be viewed as a by-product of the previous 'Cs', integrating the confidence-related strategies outlined on the following pages will also serve to reinforce them as well. By now you will be familiar with the 'PROGRESS' coaching behaviours and the manner in which you can integrate strategies to *grow* any given 'C' within your training session. Similarly your players will be accustomed to your 5C coaching approach. Therefore, by integrating these confidence strategies alongside other coaching behaviours from your 5Cs 'tool box', you should see positive gains in all areas of your players' 5C performance.

The aim of this element of the program is to further strengthen players' beliefs by highlighting gradual accomplishments during training, performing as players with positive physical presence, playing without fear, and fine tuning players' support to teammates. This will enable players to remain more mentally resilient when things don't go as expected.

As with the previous chapters, elements of your control coaching are included should you wish to reinforce them further. A summary of the confidence strategies and behaviours used within the practices is included at the end, to give you an idea of what we think are best suited for use with younger and older players. We begin by providing a worked example of how to *promote* confidence pre-training, and finish with an example of how to encourage the *self-review* process post-training.

Confidence
Coaching practices

Practice	Part of the Session				Development Phase	
	Pre Session	Warm Up	Main Session	Post Session	5-11	12-16
What is Confidence?	●	○	○	○	●	●
King of the Road	○	●	○	○	●	○
Trigger	○	●	○	○	●	○
Pass and Move	○	●	○	○	○	●
Tag Game with Corner Boxes	○	●	○	○	○	●
Running with the ball and Dribbling	○	○	●	○	●	○
Passing and Support	○	○	●	○	●	○
Deep Lying Player Game	○	○	●	○	○	●
Individual and Combined Finishing Game	○	○	●	○	○	●
5Cs Check Up	○	○	○	●	●	●

Key:

○   Does not relate to this part of the session/not appropriate for this age group

●   Relates to this part of the session/appropriate for this age group

What is Confidence?

Session Purpose

P romote

- Draw the player's attention to the value and importance of confidence
- Begin to focus the player's thoughts on the upcoming session
- Give each player the opportunity to contribute through group discussions and allowing time for feedback
- Provide the chance for the players to interact with each other in a non-threatening environment
- Start to give the players ownership over their learning by allowing the players to lead discussions and the task

R ole model

To Introduce Confidence

To introduce the players to the idea of confidence and begin to copy it during training sessions.

O wnership

Organisation: Group the players into threes or fours and ask the groups to consider the following questions. You may choose to tackle these questions over more than one pre-training session:

G row

- What do you think confidence is? Define it.
- Can you give three examples of players who you think show unshakeable confidence in their abilities?
- What behaviours do you think your chosen players show before, during and after training sessions that show they are confident players? How might they look? How might they feel? What might they be thinking?
- What behaviours might a non-confident player show before, during and after training sessions? How might they look? How might they feel? What might they be thinking?

R einforce

Review: Allow the players time to discuss their answers to these questions. Have the group nominate a spokesperson who will feedback their group's answers to the team. Based on these answers ask the players, as individuals, to select one of the behaviours from their confident player role-models to copy and show during the upcoming training session. For example, one player may elect to always want to get on the ball, or keep their head up and shoulders back to portray confidence. Their challenge therefore in the session is to unconditionally show that behaviour throughout the entire session. Afterwards review with each player how well they think they were in showing confidence.

E mpower
support

S upport
supporter

S elf-review

137

Chapter 7

Warm Up Exercise

P romote

R ole model

O wnership

G row

R einforce

E mpower support

S upport supporter

S elf-review

To Add and Emphasise Confidence

Coach Confidence: To help develop a positive and supportive environment the coach makes sure to recognise those players who are demonstrating a confident physical image, and play with a forward moving energy. The coach then positively and openly acknowledges and praises the player using first name (or nickname) terms.

YES! Football: To help develop a positive attitude in the players and highlight successes made, encourage the players to communicate to the coach and other players by shouting 'YES!' when they feel they have performed the task well.

To Reinforce Control

Choose one of the methods for this practice targeted at 'emphasising' control.

Example: Best Response Ever: Challenge the players to role model or act out the most positive response to a particular situation that you give them. Narrow down on what the correct behaviour would be in a given circumstance and give the players the opportunity to practice this.

Practice Set Up

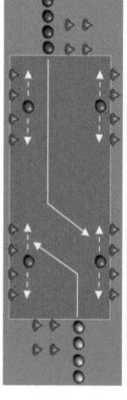

- Set up a pitch of an appropriate size for the number and age of the players
- Arrange eight 'mini gates' as shown in the diagram above
- Organise three teams of four players: four blue guards and two teams of four attackers
- The four blue 'guards' defend two of the mini gates each
- The red and yellow players stand on each side of the grid with four cones
- The red players attack the top blue guards, and the yellow players attack the bottom two blue guards

Practice Organisation

- When the coach shouts "Go!" the first red and yellow players pick up a cone and choose which of their two goals to attack
- The aim is for the red and yellow players to get past the blue guard, run through one of the two gates and put their cone down behind the gate
- If the red and yellow players achieve this they score 1 point for their team
- The blue guards get a point each time they 'tag' the attacking player
- At that point the attacking player drops their cone and joins the back of their line
- Each player takes it in turns to attack the guards and the winner is the team with the most points (cones through the gates) at the end of four attacks

138

Warm Up Exercise

Practice Set Up

- Set up a practice area of 25 yards x 25 yards for three teams of five players as shown above
- The size of the area can be amended as necessary according to the age and ability of the players in the group
- To begin the practice ask the players to move freely around the area

Practice Organisation

- One team is designated as the 'trigger' group and is given a 'trigger' movement (for example: hopping, skipping, side-stepping, running backwards)
- The other two teams are given a movement to perform in response to the trigger group
- At any time a nominated player in the 'trigger' group can 'trigger' the activity by performing their movement
- For example, the trigger group runs fast weaving in and out of the other two groups, while the remaining groups balance on one leg.
- The coach changes the activities for each group and changes the 'trigger' practice

To Add and Emphasise Confidence

Copying Confidence: To help encourage a positive attitude the players are set the task/challenge of 'training' in the session the same way as a confident player/role model would train. Place emphasis on the player's body language, self-talk, teammate support, and showing the other 4Cs.

Adjusting the Challenge: To help make manageable improvements within the session and progressing the players onto more challenging tasks, without hindering their feelings of competence, if at any point within the practice the players appear to be struggling with the new task, revert back to a previous condition that the players were comfortable with to allow for success. Alternatively you can alter the current condition so that it is easier for the players to achieve success.

Which Pitch? In a similar manner to the strategy in previous chapters, draw the player's attention to the value and importance of confidence. Pitch 1 is for those ready to train with Premiership levels of emotional confidence, show positive body language and project a confident image of themselves. Pitch 2 etc. What pitch are you ready to train on today?

To Reinforce Control

Choose one of the methods for this practice targeted at 'emphasising' control.

Example: What is Control? To enhance the value in practicing different emotional control techniques, offer players the opportunity to talk about players who they feel have excellent self-control and composure.

Chapter 7

Warm Up Exercise

P romote	
R ole model	
O wnership	
G row	
R einforce	
E mpower support	
S upport supporter	
S elf-review	

To Add and Emphasise Confidence

Set a Goal with "Yes!" Football: To help the players feel a sense of achievement and develop a positive attitude, set the players realistic but challenging goals to achieve during the practice. For example, can the players make each pass forwards? How quickly can they move the ball from each of the boxes? Can they beat this time? Can they vary their types and distances of their passes? Encourage the players to communicate to the coach and other players by shouting 'YES!' when they feel they have performed the task well.

Stepping it Up: To keep challenging the players and building on their achievements within the practice, progressively increase the difficulty of the practice. For example, add opposition, reduce the target areas to pass into, prescribe a set amount of passes to make under pressure.

To Reinforce Control

Choose one of the methods targeted at 'adding in' control.

Example: Body Language and Self-talk: The players in the target zone focuses on their breathing, body language and positive self-talk prior to re-entering the practice.

Practice Set Up

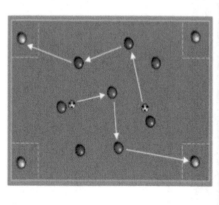

- Organise a pitch of 25 yards x 15 yards
- Set up four small 'target' boxes in the corners of the pitch
- Split the group into three teams of four
- One group of four is positioned in the target boxes (yellow)
- The remaining groups of four (red and blue) spread themselves out in the middle of the grid
- Each of the middle groups have a football each

Practice Organisation

- The middle red and blue teams look to pass the ball between them
- The aim is to pass the ball into a yellow target player in each corner until they have passed the ball to all four corners
- Each player must touch the ball before it is played into a corner
- The teams can pass into the corners in any order they wish
- Both groups are aiming to do this faster than the other group

Tag Game with Corner Boxes

| Warm Up Exercise | Youth Development Phase |

Practice Set Up

- Set up an area of 25 yards x 25 yards is organised with four corner boxes marked as shown in the diagram
- Amend the size of the area as necessary according to the age and ability of the players in the group
- Organise three teams of four players, with one team designated as the 'tagging' team (in the diagram above the yellow team has been designated the 'tagging' team)
- The practice starts in the central area

Practice Organisation

- The tagging team are given 60 seconds to try and tag as many players as possible
- If a player is tagged, they must go to one of the squares and perform the designated activity
- Once completed they can re-join the practice
- Swap the tagging team over after 60 seconds
- The challenge for the tagging team is to see if they can send every attacker to one of the activity squares in 60 seconds

To Add and Emphasise Confidence

P romote

Peer "Yes!" Football: Encourage players to support and verbally acknowledge teammates who look confident or show confidence in their actions and skill executions (e.g. looking to beat a defender 1v1). Ask the players to openly say something like: "Yes! Jack's on it – great effort!" Allow the players to choose what they say, but this is a powerful way of developing a supportive and confidence climate.

R ole model

Copying Confidence: To help encourage a positive attitude the players are set the task/challenge of 'training' in the session the same way as a confident player/role model would train. Place emphasis on the player's body language, self-talk, teammate support, and showing the other 4Cs. You may also extend this to role modelling their favourite 'confident' players' skill to practice within the session.

O wnership

To Reinforce Control

G row

R einforce

Choose one of the methods targeted at 'emphasising' control.

E mpower support

Example: Individual Rules of Engagement: Before re-entering the players must give a sign to the coach, such as a 'thumbs up' or shout "I'm Back!" as an indication to the coach the player is ready to re-enter the practice.

S upport supporter

S elf-review

141

Main Session Exercise

To Add and Emphasise Confidence

Stepping it Up: Keep challenging the players and building on their achievements within the practice by progressively increasing the difficulty of the practice. For example, the players have to add changes of speed, direction and body feints as they move through the inner square; add 2 defenders into the inner square for the players to dribble past; remove the inner square so the defenders are free to move around the square, so the attackers have to move to get free in order to receive the pass, or once the defenders win the ball they have to dribble/run the ball out of larger grid.

Adjusting the Challenge: Help the players make manageable improvements within the session, and progress onto more challenging tasks without hindering their feelings of competence. If at any point within the practice the players appear to be struggling with the new task, revert back to a previous condition that the players were comfortable with to allow for success. Alternatively you can alter the current condition so that it is easier for the players to achieve success.

P romote

R ole model

O wnership

G row

R einforce

E mpower
support

S upport
supporter

S elf-review

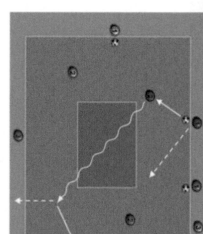

Practice Set Up

- Organise an area of 25 yards x 25 yards, with an inner square of 8 yards x 8 yards
- Arrange three groups of three players as shown in the diagram
- One ball per group
- The practice starts with two players from each group working outside the large square, with the other player in the area between the two squares

Practice Organisation

- In each group: Player 1 passes to player 2, who runs the ball across and out of the inner square
- Player 2 then passes to player 3 and exits the playing area
- Player 1 now moves into the square and receives a pass from player 3
- Player 1 then runs the ball across the and out of the inner square and passes to player 2
- Repeat the exercise with player 3 receiving the ball from player 2
- All groups work at the same time

Passing and Support

| Main Session Exercise | Foundation Phase |

To Add and Emphasise Confidence

Stepping it Up: To keep challenging the players and building on their achievements within the practice, progressively increase the difficulty of the practice. For example, ask the players to use their non-dominant foot only, introduce more defenders, reducing the playing area, or removing the 'safety zone'.

Set a Goal: To help the players feel a sense of achievement and develop a positive attitude, challenge the players to see how many successful passes can the player make? Can they beat it next time? Or, how many successful, consecutive passes can the players make? Can they beat it next time? You may wish to time the players and see how many successful passes they can make in a given time. Can the player beat it next time?

Practice Set Up

- Organise two squares: an outside square of 15 yards x 15 yards, and an inner square of 12 yards x 12 yards, giving a 3 yards "safety zone"
- Four attackers play against 1 defender
- 2 target players support the attackers on the outside of the inner grid

Practice Organisation

- The attackers in the inner square look to pass the ball accurately from one of the outside target players to the other and back again
- If under pressure, the attackers can dribble the ball into the "safety zone" where he cannot be tackled
- If this happens, one of the target players swaps places and joins in the inner square
- If the defender wins the ball they switch places with the player who lost possession

P romote

R ole model

O wnership

G row

R einforce

E mpower support

S upport supporter

S elf-review

143

Main Session Exercise

To Add and Emphasise Confidence

P romote	**Adjusting the Challenge:** To help the players make manageable improvements within the session without hindering their feelings of competence, add one or two neutral players into the middle third to overload in favour of the team in possession and ensure the players gain success early in the practice.
R ole model	
O wnership	
G row	**Stepping it Up:** To keep challenging the players and building on their achievements within the practice, progressively increase the difficulty of the practice. For example, allow the 'deep lying' player to show the confidence to travel out of the defensive third into the middle third. The 'deep lying' player must retreat back if the team loses possession; allow the players to rotate in and out of the 'safety zone' so that all players get the opportunity to get comfortable on the ball; allow the defending team to put pressure on the 'deep lying' player, or the points a team gets for scoring a goal is equivalent to the number of passes the team makes. For example, if a team makes 5 passes before scoring, they 'bank' 5 points.
R einforce	
E mpower support	**Peer "Yes!" Football:** Encourage players to support and verbally acknowledge teammates who look confident or show confidence in their actions and skill executions (e.g. looking to beat a defender 1v1). Ask the players to openly say something like: "Yes! Jack's on it – great effort!' Allow the players to choose what they say, but this is a powerful way of developing a supportive and confidence climate
S upport supporter	
S elf-review	

Practice Set Up

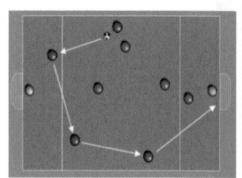

- Set up a pitch 30 yards x 20 yards split into thirds, with the outer zones of 5 yards x 20 yards and goals at opposite ends of the pitch
- Organise 10 players so that there is a 3v3 inside the central square and 1 defender and 1 goalkeeper each in the outer zones
- The players must remain in their zones

Practice Organisation

- The two teams aim to score in the opponents goal by shooting from the middle third
- The team in possession should use their 'deep lying' player to retain possession
- The 'deep lying' player plays in the teams own outer zone, which acts as a 'safety zone'
- When the ball is in the 'safety zone' the defending team cannot put pressure on the 'deep lying' player and most remain in the middle third
- **Note:** The emphasis of this practice can be altered to focus on building a goalkeepers' confidence in receiving back passes, and distributing from defence. To do this remove the deep lying play maker from the outer 'safety zone'

Individual and Combined Finishing

Main Session Exercise

To Add and Emphasise Confidence

Stepping It Up: To keep challenging the players and building on their achievements within the practice, progressively increase the difficulty of the practice. For example, encourage the attacker to add body feints/fakes before shooting; limit the number of touches the attacker has, or add defenders to the practice to defend 1v1 (facing, from the side, prevent turning).

Set a Goal: To help the players feel a sense of achievement and develop a positive attitude, ask the attacking players how many shots on target, or goals, they believe they can achieve out of 10 shots? If they are successful, can the beat it next time? Ask the defending players how many attacks they can stop successfully out of 10 attempts? If they are successful, can they beat it next time?

Coach Confidence: To help develop a positive and supportive environment the coach makes sure to recognise those players who are demonstrating a confident physical image, and play with a forward moving energy. The coach then positively and openly acknowledging and praises the player using first name (or nickname) terms.

P romote

R ole model

O wnership

G row

R einforce

E mpower
support

S upport
supporter

S elf-review

Practice Set Up

- Use the penalty box and goal
- Position two servers either side of the goal and two servers 10 yards outside the penalty box
- Each of the servers has a supply of football
- Two attackers are positioned on the edge of the box, with the goalkeeper defending the goal

Practice Organisation

- The practice starts with the ball being played diagonally into one of the attackers, who turns and shoots at goal
- Immediately a server from the goal line feeds a ball in for the same striker to shoot
- The sequence is repeated with the other striker
- Rotate attackers and servers after a pre-determined number of strikes at goal

Chapter 7

P romote

R ole model

O wnership

G row

R einforce

E mpower
support

S upport
supporter

S elf-review

Session Purpose

- To 'close' the session down appropriately
- Work with the players to set a future direction for the next confidence training session
- To collaborate with the player's to review the quality of team confidence strategy use
- Provide the players with the opportunity to self-reflect on their own confidence performance and judge what they have learnt from the training session

To Review Confidence

Allow the players to assess how well they have applied each of the 5Cs within the training session.

Organisation: Gather the players together after the session and run through each of the 5Cs, allowing the players to offer their views of how each 'C' was performed within the team, and/or as an individual. Probe the answers the players provide to specifically find out which elements the players thought they did well at, which they believe could be improved and in which situations. For example, you may wish to ask all or some of the following questions:

- How committed were we today? How well did we communicate today? How focused were we today? How well did we remain in control of our emotions today? How well did we show our confidence today?
- Which 'C' was a particular strength of ours today?
- Which 'C' could we show more of in the next session?
- Which part(s) of the session were our 'Cs' at their best? Why might this have been?
- Which part(s) of the session were our 'Cs' not at their best? What can we do next time to make sure we remain consistent?
- Which of the 'Cs' did you show the most today? How effective was it?
- Which of the 'Cs' did you show the least today? What can you do in the next session to use that 'C' more?

It might be useful for you, or your players, to write down the answers you receive from these questions. The responses can then be referred to at the start of the next session to continue to promote your player's 5C use, and set goals to achieve within that session.

Confidence: Summary

It is widely accepted that success breeds confidence. Those players with the greatest confidence are often the ones most likely to seek ways of making positive improvements, are unafraid of doing so, and feel unburdened by minor hiccups. They ultimately perform better. However being confident is not simply about being good at a skill. Whilst this undoubtedly does act as a key source of confidence, your role as a coach in developing confident players must, and does, go beyond that.

As we have outlined earlier, a player's confidence can be positively influenced by well-developed commitment, communication, concentration and control skills. When these four 'Cs' are functioning well, a player's confidence is also likely to be elevated. However, the relationship can be cyclical in that the greater the consistency of this confidence, the more likely the player is to exhibit the four 'Cs' in training and match performances.

Hopefully whilst looking through the example practices over the previous pages you will have noticed a conscious attempt at creating opportunities for your players to: achieve and feel successful at every step, 'banking' confidence as they progress; receive unconditional support and gain feedback from multiple sources (including peers); and to play with a sense of challenge and forward-moving expression that literally encourages confident, courageous interactions and responses between players.

Coaching strategies and behaviours summary

Strategy	Targeting Confidence			Development Phase	
	Attitude	Support	Accomplishments	5-11	12-16
Adjusting the Challenge	○	○	●	●	●
Coach Confidence	○	●	●	●	●
Copying Confidence	●	○	○	●	●
Peer "Yes!" Football	●	●	○	●	●
Set a Goal	●	○	●	●	●
Stepping it Up	○	○	●	●	●
Which Pitch?	●	○	○	●	●
"Yes!" Football	●	○	●	●	●

Key:

○   Not the focus of this strategy/not appropriate for this age group

●   Focus of this exercise/appropriate for this age group

8

Developing the 5C Coaching Climate

Having reached this stage and outlined the specific behaviours, skills, and strategies of the 5Cs, as well as how to cultivate each within a training session, we switch our focus towards providing you with an example structure of a 5Cs training program. Through this we enable you to see how your work may be integrated over the course of a twelve month period. An ongoing element to this will be how you review and reflect on each 5C session you conduct, and how these evaluations feed back into your training programme. Therefore we also include a review sheet for each of the 'Cs' in order for you to consistently self-reflect on your 5C coaching practice and help drive the process of seeking constant improvements in your players.

Whilst all the 'Cs' are interactive, as we have maintained throughout the book, we believe the easiest way to introduce and teach them is separately. As you will have noticed, there are elements and strategies of one 'C' that can easily crossover into another 'C', but coaching one 'C' at a time will ensure that your players learn and improve the necessary behaviours and responses at the appropriate times. However, regardless of which 'C' you may be working on, it is useful to be aware of the fact that you will be affecting each 'C', whether intentionally or not, during players' training sessions, such is the interactive nature of the 5Cs (see the 5C Coaching Climate diagram in the Confidence chapter as a reminder of how the 5Cs fit together).

5C Seasonal Coaching Plan

In order to get the full benefit of the practices and strategies outlined in the previous chapters, they need to be repeated on a regular basis. With regular and structured work that is reinforced at every opportunity within your training sessions, you will find a shift in the use and ownership of the 5Cs behaviours and responses. This requires a long-term commitment to plan in advance what you want to achieve. Just like learning to pass a ball accurately with the correct technique and with the right weight time and time again, being able to show the skills and responses of the 5Cs in every training session and in every match takes time. Doing one session that emphasises the principles of commitment or concentration is not going to automatically produce the ultimate committed or focused player!

Over the following pages we will outline an example of a twelve month 5Cs coaching plan to help you integrate the 5Cs within your coaching over the season. This plan has been specifically written with the Youth Development Phase in mind (i.e., 12-16 years old) but is easily adaptable for players in the Foundation Phase (i.e., 8-11 years old). The twelve month plan is broken down into three phases: a one month 'pre-season', a ten month 'competitive season' and a one month 'transition phase'. To ensure a continued and systematic progression within one 'C' and between the 'Cs', the twelve months have been split into two five month cycles. Each cycle follows the suggested development course starting with commitment, moving on to communication, then concentration and control, before concluding with confidence. Each monthly plan outlines a set of aims for the month that look to introduce and build the foundation of that 'C' within the first month, and then develop it further in the second cycle.

The weekly content itself is built around including a 'C'- related warm-up, in order to not only warm up physically but also mentally for the session. This is then supplemented with one sole practice geared towards developing the 'C'. In this way we do not detract from the other areas you may wish to focus on in your training sessions. However this does not preclude you from using the strategies outlined throughout this book in other parts of your session if you wish. In fact as you and your players become more familiar and confident in all the 'C' strategies, conducting practices focused solely on a 'C' may become unnecessary, and using the strategies within your sessions as you see fit may be more appropriate.

At the end of each training month we encourage you to include a practice of your choice from the previous month's 'C' coaching. In doing so you continue to value the continued importance of the 'Cs' and shape your players' views of them. You further enhance their attention to using the strategies and showing consistent 'C'-related behaviours month to month.

As an additional element to the programme we have included two 'reflection' months at the end of each five month cycle. These months are built-in to allow you to conduct training sessions that allow the players to practice utilising their 5Cs without being prompted. This is not to say that you shouldn't work directly on the 'Cs' if you wish. If you feel your players would benefit from some further coaching on one of the 'Cs' then this one month gap is an ideal time to do that. However we do acknowledge that coaches will be doing things in training that affect the players' 5Cs whether intentionally or not, therefore there is no necessity on the coaches' part to formally conduct sessions focused on a particular 'C' during these months.

As with the training practices that appear in this book, the twelve month 5Cs plan is merely a possible way in which each 'C' could be organised and structured over a twelve month period. We encourage you to personalise and adapt these plans to suit your team and club environment as you see necessary. It will, no doubt, take some time to plan and put together a structured development plan, however we believe that this will be a worthwhile endeavour.

5C 12 Month Plan: Overview

Seasonal Aims/Objectives
- To introduce and develop the 5Cs of commitment, communication, concentration, control and confidence at an individual and team level
- To integrate the 5Cs alongside the technical, tactical and physical syllabus of the team

Cycle 1

Cycle Aims/Objectives
- Establish a positive learning environment to foster player development
- Promote the importance of the 5Cs amongst the players
- Introduce and teach the 5Cs specific to the age group
- Review the effectiveness in implementing the 5Cs on an individual and team level to inform content for cycle 2

Months:	July	August	September	October	November	December
Phase of Season:	Pre Season		Competitive Season			
Training Weeks:						
The 'C':	Commitment	Communication	Concentration	Control	Confidence	Reflection

Cycle 2

Cycle Aims/Objectives
- Build a 'no fear of failure' environment to foster player development
- Continue to value the importance of the 5Cs as players and coaches
- Develop and progress the 5C behaviours and responses of the players
- Review the effectiveness in implementing the 5Cs on an individual and team level to inform content for next year

Months:	January	February	March	April	May	June
Phase of Season:	Competitive Season					Transition
Training Weeks:						
The 'C':	Commitment	Communication	Concentration	Control	Confidence	Reflection

Pre Season

July

Commitment

Aims/Objectives

- Develop a work ethic amongst the players/team
- Develop a task orientated climate amongst the team
- Establish a positive learning environment
- Value the importance of developing new skills at all times (more effort equals more improvement)
- Establish regular avenues of feedback with the players

Week 1	Week 2	Week 3	Week 4
'C' Warm Up: Pass and Move	**'C' Warm Up:** Pass and Move	**'C' Warm Up:** Tag Game with Corner Boxes	**'C' Warm Up:** Tag Game with Corner Boxes
Commitment Exercise: Breakout Game	**Commitment Exercise:** Breakout Game	**Commitment Exercise:** 2v2 Shooting Practice	**Commitment Exercise:** 2v2 Shooting Practice

Checks

- Have the players set themselves goals for the coming sessions/weeks?
- Have the players communicated those goals to the coach?
- Are the players engaged in the task/drill/game/challenge?
- Does the practice allow the players to feel in control of their learning?
- Does the practice allow the players to make their own decisions?
- Does the practice foster feelings of competence in the player?
- Does the exercise allow the players to socially interact with one another?

How do I plan to Promote Role Model Ownership Grow Reinforce Empower peer support Support the support Self-review this C?

Competitive Season

August

Communication

Aims/Objectives

- Develop verbal and non-verbal communication skills with the players
- Develop the players' ability to 'send' and 'receive' information effectively
- Establish what is good and bad communication
- Introduce a 'HELPA' philosophy to the players regarding our communication

Week 1	Week 2	Week 3	Week 4
'C' Warm Up: Pass and Move	**'C' Warm Up:** Pass and Move	**'C' Warm Up:** Tag Game with Corner Boxes	**'C' Warm Up:** Tag Game with Corner Boxes
Communication Exercise: Communication Focused Match	**Communication Exercise:** Communication Focused Match	**Communication Exercise:** Defending as a Defending Unit	**Communication Exercise:** Defending as a Defending Unit
			Commitment Exercise: Choose one commitment exercise from previous month to re-affirm the value and importance of commitment

Checks

- Does the practice allow the players to practice positive communication?
- Are the players being encouraged to become self-aware of their strengths and limitations in communicating?
- Is the practice providing enough opportunities for players to work on their communication limitations?
- Does the practice allow the players to create solid working relationships?
- Does the practice challenge the players to communicate with one another?
- Are the players who provide negative communication shown the effects of their communication and shown positive alternatives?

How do I plan to Promote Role Model Ownership Grow Reinforce Empower peer support Support the support Self-review this C?

Competitive Season

September

Concentration

Aims/Objectives

- Develop the players narrow-internal, narrow-external, broad-internal and broad-external attentional styles
- Develop the players ability to switch between these attentional channels
- Train the players 'mental effort' and stretch their attention span by linking mental and physical effort
- Develop the players ability to focus and refocus at key moments during a game
- Help the players appropriately manage their concentration through the use of 'trigger' words
- Teach the players how to cope with distractions

Week 1	Week 2	Week 3	Week 4
'C' Warm Up: Pass and Move	**'C' Warm Up:** Pass and Move	**'C' Warm Up:** Tag Game with Corner Boxes	**'C' Warm Up:** Tag Game with Corner Boxes
Concentration Exercise: Trigger Word Small Sided Game	**Concentration Exercise:** Trigger Word Small Sided Game	**Concentration Exercise:** Support Play Possession Practice	**Concentration Exercise:** Support Play Possession Practice
			Communication Exercise: Choose one communication exercise from previous month to re-affirm the value and importance of communication

Checks

- Does the practice allow the players to practice their 'senses' and attend to relevant 'cues' and process task relevant information?
- Are the players aware of those relevant 'cues' to which they should be attending for different situations?
- Does the practice stretch the players' attention span?
- Does the practice train and test the players' attentional channels?
- Does the practice allow the players concentration to be tested and trained by using distraction and game-like situations/scenarios?

How do I plan to Promote Role Model Ownership Grow Reinforce Empower peer support Support the support Self-review this C?

155

Competitive Season

October

Control

Aims/Objectives

- Highlight the importance of emotions, thoughts and feelings on performance and what are and are not acceptable behaviours and emotional responses
- Introduce relaxation and readying methods to the players (for example, breathing techniques, physical presence and self-talk)
- Create a supportive on-pitch climate that unites the team to deal with challenges and errors
- Develop the players ability to manage and control their emotions, thoughts and feelings
- Develop the players coping skills to bounce back from testing situations where things consistently go against them

Week 1	Week 2	Week 3	Week 4
'C' Warm Up: Pass and Move	**'C' Warm Up:** Pass and Move	**'C' Warm Up:** Tag Game with Corner Boxes	**'C' Warm Up:** Tag Game with Corner Boxes
Communication Exercise: Bad Refereeing Game	**Communication Exercise:** Bad Refereeing Game	**Communication Exercise:** Courage Under Fire	**Communication Exercise:** Courage Under Fire
			Concentration Exercise: Choose one concentration exercise from previous month to re-affirm the value and importance of concentration

Checks

- Have the players turned up to training in an appropriate emotional state and ready to train?
- Does the practice allow the players to practice key control strategies?
- Do the players have appropriate error management routines?
- Does the coach ensure the players are 'emotionally ready' for the next practice exercise following a break?
- Are the players emotionally supporting each other?
- Does the practice test the players' emotional responses in game-like situations/scenarios both in adversity and when things are going well?

How do I plan to **Promote Role Model Ownership Grow Reinforce Empower** peer support **Support** the support **Self-review** this C?

Competitive Season

November

Confidence

Aims/Objectives

- Educate players in what confidence is, how a confident player behaves, and how they develop it
- Develop a supportive coach/teammate environment that allows players to feel no fear of reprisal for failure
- Develop the player's self-belief in their skills through gradual goal progressions, positive feedback and a strengths focus.
- Encourage the players to tackle new challenges and persist in the face of difficulty
- Continue to develop and incorporate important features from the previous 4 'Cs'

Week 1	Week 2	Week 3	Week 4
'C' Warm Up: Pass and Move	**'C' Warm Up:** Pass and Move	**'C' Warm Up:** Tag Game with Corner Boxes	**'C' Warm Up:** Tag Game with Corner Boxes
Confidence Exercise: Deep Lying Player Game	**Confidence Exercise:** Deep Lying Player Game	**Confidence Exercise:** Individual and Combined Finishing	**Confidence Exercise:** Individual and Combined Finishing

Control Exercise: Choose one control exercise from previous month to re-affirm the value and importance of control

Checks

- Have the players made a list of the positive accomplishments they've achieved to date?
- Have the players communicated their previous accomplishments?
- Are practices progressive, moving from simple to complex activities to promote gradual accomplishments?
- Do practices allow players to showcase their strengths (e.g., favourite drills; feel good practices)?
- Do the player's always want the ball during the practice?
- Are the players looking confident throughout the practice session and encouraged to practice a resilient physical presence?
- Are players supporting each other and influencing each other's attitudes positively

How do I plan to Promote Role Model Ownership Grow Reinforce Empower peer support Support the support Self-review this C?

Competitive Season

December

Reflection Month

Aims/Objectives
- To allow the players to work on their 5C skills and behaviours unprompted
- To consolidate and work on areas for development from the previous cycle
- To assess the players current use of the 5Cs in order to help inform work in the next cycle

	Week 1	Week 2	Week 3	Week 4
Warm Up:	'C' Warm Up:	'C' Warm Up:	'C' Warm Up:	'C' Warm Up:
Main Exercise:	Main Exercise:	Main Exercise:	Main Exercise:	Main Exercise:

Checks
- Are the practices providing the players with an opportunity to show the coach what they have learnt?
- Are the players showing the skills and behaviours they've been taught without guidance?
- Are identified areas for improvement being worked on within the session?
- Have areas for improvement been identified from previous sessions by the coach and with the players?
- Have the players been given the opportunity to suggest 5C areas they wish to work on?
- Are the training sessions being monitored and reflected upon to influence the work being carried out in the next cycle?

How do I plan to **P**romote **R**ole Model **O**wnership **G**row **R**einforce **E**mpower peer support **S**upport the support **S**elf-review the Cs?

Competitive Season

January

Commitment

Aims/Objectives

- Maintain and develop the work ethic amongst the players/team, with the player showing a desire to work on making self-improvements
- Maintain the task orientated climate amongst the team
- Maintain a positive learning environment
- Continue to value the importance of developing new skills at all times encouraging the players to take responsibility for their own improvement
- Maintain and develop regular avenues of feedback with the players, identifying where the player can make improvements

Week 1	Week 2	Week 3	Week 4
'C' Warm Up: Tag Game with Corner Boxes	**'C' Warm Up:** Pass and Move	**'C' Warm Up:** Tag Game with Corner Boxes	**'C' Warm Up:** Pass and Move
Commitment Exercise: 2v2 Shooting Practice	**Commitment Exercise:** Breakout Game	**Commitment Exercise:** 2v2 Shooting Practice	**Commitment Exercise:** Breakout Game

Checks

- Have the players set themselves goals for the coming sessions/weeks?
- Have the player communicated those goals to the coach?
- Are the players engaged in the task/drill/game/challenge?
- Does the practice allow the players to feel in control of their learning?
- Does the practice allow the players to make their own decisions?
- Does the practice foster feelings of competence in the player?
- Does the exercise allow the players to socially interact with one another?

How do I plan to Promote Role Model Ownership Grow Reinforce Empower peer support Support the support Self-review this C?

Competitive Season

February

Communication

Aims/Objectives

- Improve verbal and non-verbal communication skills with the players, improving clarity and specificity of instructions to teammates
- Develop further the players' ability to 'send' and 'receive' information effectively, showing stronger evidence of listening skills and confidence in supporting and encouraging teammates
- Reinforce what is good and bad communication
- Continue to develop and strengthen the teams' 'HELPA' philosophy and look towards using it to develop leadership on and off the pitch

Week 1	Week 2	Week 3	Week 4
'C' Warm Up: Tag Game with Corner Boxes	**'C' Warm Up:** Pass and Move	**'C' Warm Up:** Tag Game with Corner Boxes	**'C' Warm Up:** Pass and Move
Communication Exercise: Defending as a Defensive Unit	**Communication Exercise:** Communication Focused Match	**Communication Exercise:** Defending as a Defensive Unit	**Communication Exercise:** Communication Focused Match
			Commitment Exercise: Choose one commitment exercise from previous month to re-affirm the value and importance of commitment

Checks

- Does the practice allow the players to practice positive communication?
- Are the players being encouraged to become self-aware of their strengths and limitations in communicating?
- Is the practice providing enough opportunities for players to work on their communication limitations?
- Does the practice allow the players to create solid working relationships?
- Does the practice challenge the players to communicate with one another?
- Are the players who provide negative communication shown the effects of their communication and shown positive alternatives?

How do I plan to Promote Role Model Ownership Grow Reinforce Empower peer support Support the support Self-review this C?

Competitive Season

March

Concentration

Aims/Objectives

- Continue to develop the players narrow-internal, narrow-external, broad-internal and broad-external attentional styles within their specific roles on the pitch
- Continue to develop the players ability to switch between these attentional channels within their role on the pitch
- Train the players 'mental effort' and stretch their attention span by linking mental and physical effort
- Improve the players ability to concentrate at key moments during a game, especially moments of transition from attack to defence and defence to attack
- Help the players appropriately manage their concentration through the use of 'trigger' words in order to better read the game
- Improve how the players cope with distractions

Week 1	Week 2	Week 3	Week 4
'C' Warm Up: Tag Game with Corner Boxes	**'C' Warm Up:** Tag Game with Corner Boxes	**'C' Warm Up:** Tag Game with Corner Boxes	**'C' Warm Up:** Pass and Move

Concentration Exercise: Support Play Possession Practice	**Concentration Exercise:** Trigger Word Small Sided Game	**Concentration Exercise:** Support Play Possession Practice	**Concentration Exercise:** Trigger Word Small Sided Game

Checks

- Does the practice allow the players to practice their 'senses' and attend to relevant 'cues' and process task relevant information?
- Are the players aware of those relevant 'cues' to which they should be attending for different situations?
- Does the practice stretch the players' attention span?
- Does the practice train and test the players' attentional channels?
- Does the practice allow the players concentration to be tested and trained by using distraction and game-like situations/scenarios?

How do I plan to Promote Role Model Ownership Grow Reinforce Empower peer support Support the support Self-review this C?

Competitive Season

April

Control

Aims/Objectives

- Develop further the supportive pitch climate that unites the team to deal with challenges and errors
- Progress the relaxation methods used by the players (for example, breathing techniques, body language and self-talk)
- Continue to highlight the importance of emotions, thoughts and feelings on performance
- Monitor the behaviour and emotional responses of the players
- Improve the players ability to manage and control their emotions, thoughts and feelings
- Increase the players coping skills to bounce back from testing situations where things go against them

Week 1	Week 2	Week 3	Week 4
'C' Warm Up: Pass and Move	**'C' Warm Up:** Tag Game with Corner Boxes	**'C' Warm Up:** Pass and Move	**'C' Warm Up:** Tag Game with Corner Boxes
Control Exercise: Courage Under Fire	**Control Exercise:** Bad Refereeing Game	**Control Exercise:** Courage Under Fire	**Control Exercise:** Bad Refereeing Game
			Concentration Exercise: Choose one concentration exercise from previous month to re-affirm the value and importance of concentration

Checks

- Have the players turned up to training in an appropriate emotional state and ready to train?
- Does the practice allow the players to practice key control strategies?
- Do the players have appropriate error management routines?
- Does the coach ensure the players are 'emotionally ready' for the next practice exercise following a break?
- Are the players emotionally supporting each other?
- Does the practice test the players' emotional responses in game-like situations/scenarios both in adversity and when things are going well?

How do I plan to **P**romote **R**ole Model **O**wnership **G**row **R**einforce **E**mpower peer support **S**upport the support **S**elf-review this C?

Competitive Season

May

Confidence

Aims/Objectives

- Reinforce through player discussion their understanding of what confidence is, how a confident player behaves, and how they develop it
- Establish an environment that is free from a 'fear of failure' and encourage the players to mimic a 'without fear' approach in their overall play
- Develop the players' self-belief in their skills and demonstrate a positive attitude to training and matches
- Encourage the players to tackle new challenges and persist in the face of difficulty
- Continue to develop and incorporate important features from the previous 4 Cs so that players are influencing each other's beliefs

Week 1	Week 2	Week 3	Week 4
'C' Warm Up: Pass and Move	**'C' Warm Up:** Tag Game with Corner Boxes	**'C' Warm Up:** Pass and Move	**'C' Warm Up:** Tag Game with Corner Boxes
Confidence Exercise: Individual and Combined Finishing	**Confidence Exercise:** Deep Lying Player Game	**Confidence Exercise:** Individual and Combined Finishing	**Confidence Exercise:** Deep Lying Player Game

Control Exercise: Choose one control exercise from previous month to re-affirm the value and importance of control

Checks

- Have the players made a list of the positive accomplishments they've achieved to date?
- Have the players communicated their previous accomplishments?
- Are practices progressive, moving from simple to complex activities to promote gradual accomplishments?
- Do practices allow players to showcase their strengths (e.g., favourite drills; feel good practices)?
- Do the player's always want the ball during the practice?
- Are the players looking confident throughout the practice session and encouraged to practice a resilient physical presence?
- Are players supporting each other and influencing each other's attitudes positively

How do I plan to Promote Role Model Ownership Grow Reinforce Empower peer support Support the support Self-review this C?

Competitive Season

June

Reflection Month

Aims/Objectives

- To allow the players to work on their 5C skills and behaviours unprompted
- To consolidate and work on areas for development from the previous cycle
- To assess the players current use of the 5Cs in order to help inform work for the following season

	Week 1	Week 2	Week 3	Week 4
Warm Up:	'C' Warm Up:	'C' Warm Up:	'C' Warm Up:	'C' Warm Up:
Main Exercise:		Main Exercise:	Main Exercise:	Main Exercise:

Checks

- Are the practices providing the players with an opportunity to show the coach what they have learnt and testing their ability to use the 5Cs?
- Are the players showing the skills and behaviours they've been taught without guidance more coherently?
- Are identified areas for improvement being worked on within the session in game-like situations?

- Have areas for improvement been identified from previous sessions by the coach and with the players?
- Have the players been given the opportunity to suggest 5C areas they wish to work on?
- Are the training sessions being monitored and reflected upon to influence the work being carried out in the next cycle?

How do I plan to **P**romote **R**ole Model **O**wnership **G**row **R**einforce **E**mpower peer support **S**upport the support **S**elf-review the Cs?

The 5C Coaching Review Process

You've just finished your first training session incorporating the 5Cs and started implementing the first 'C' of the 5Cs with your players:

- How did it go?
- What went well?
- Why did it go well?
- What elements didn't go as planned?
- Why didn't they go as well as you would have liked?
- What could you do that would make the session even better next time?

The chances are that these questions, or ones similar, are among the first things you asked yourself as you began your journey home after training. In fact you may have even begun asking yourself these questions during the session: "How's this practice going?", "Is this working how I wanted it to work?", "How can I change this to help progress the session further?" Sound familiar? That is because you are already engaging in the process of evaluation and self-reflection about the successes of your session, and trying to identify areas that need improvement.

By this stage you will have learnt many new skills and strategies to add to those you already possess as a coach, all focused on effectively teaching psychological skills to your players. The more you consciously go out on the training pitch and practice using this new knowledge, the more confident and comfortable you and your players will be with it. Therefore, in line with the core commitment behaviours from earlier in the chapter, coaches themselves should also be concerned with the development of their own competence in delivering psychological skills coaching to their players. Just as you expect your players to be committed in their approach to training and matches, so you too must demonstrate that same level of commitment when it comes to looking back at the successes and areas for improvement from your training sessions.

By doing a more formal evaluation you will strengthen the learning from your sessions. You will have a sense of what behaviours and responses were taken on-board by the players and which strategies worked best for you to bring about player learning. Unfortunately, many coaches believe the only way they learn to be better coaches is through the training sessions they put on. The more training sessions, the better coach they will become. However, simply acquiring these experiences does not guarantee competence. It is the integration of this experience and knowledge in a meaningful way that promotes learning and in turn creates a better coach. You most likely do not coach the same way now as you did 10 years ago. Along your coaching journey you will have discarded elements to your coaching that you no longer felt valuable, or decided on new ways to approach problems to help your players learn more effectively. So, in this regard, being able to self-evaluate is a major learning tool.

An effective 5C coach is one who reflects on the application of the 5Cs in their coaching on training and matchday.

Using the review sheets we've included over the following pages you can start to clarify the thoughts and feelings you have about each of your 5C coaching sessions. These reviews aim to help clarify the areas that you felt you and your team were strong at and which areas you feel you and your team can make improvements on. If you make the conscious effort to habitually review the success of your training sessions, you will be able to track not only your players' improvements in their 5C skills, but you are also growing confidence in using these behaviours and strategies successfully.

Although such reviews can seem onerous to carry out session after session, it is well worth the time to help improve your confidence in delivering the 5Cs. As a knock on effect you will be able to see your players grow more psychologically aware and more proficient in their abilities to implement the behaviours and responses of the 5Cs effectively. Model coaches often approach this as a solitary endeavour. They may keep a diary related to their experiences or they may simply conduct a mindful evaluation within the first 24 hours after training. Their approach to evaluating their sessions is usually systematic and integrated into their everyday practice. It often involves both technical evaluations and personal considerations along with a willingness to accept responsibility for the impact of their choices. As such, top coaches are willing to assume responsibility for their decisions. Sometimes strategies will work out well, while at other times they will not. Reflective coaches consider their decisions and accept the consequences of those decisions, making adjustments to their future choices. How well you focus on these actions will essentially determine how productive your last training session has been, or whether lessons are forgotten after a couple of days.

Each of the reviews for the individual 'Cs' follows a similar format. The coach is asked to consider their use of key coaching behaviours and strategies aimed at facilitating a particular 'C'. Each behaviour or strategy is self-rated from 1 to 5 and enables the coach to quantify their sessions on a session-by-session or week-by-week basis. There is also room for additional comments that may help in fully reflecting on the session and drive future progress in integrating the 5Cs into training sessions. We have also included a review sheet for the 'reflection' month periods. This review is much more open-ended than the individual 'C' reviews. As such, the coach is encouraged to consider more thoughtfully the development that has occurred amongst your players, and plan ahead to the areas that still need further development, as well as those where further progress can be made in the next cycle.

Commitment Session Evaluation

Answer the questions below circling the closest and most honest response. Then add any examples and comments to the question that you feel will help you improve in that area for your next session. The rating scale is as follows: **1** = Not at all; **2** = Infrequent/Poor; **3** = Moderately well; **4** = Quite well/Appropriately; **5** = Very well/At all appropriate times

Question	1	2	3	4	5
How well did I give equal recognition to players for successful outcomes and for high effort?	1	2	3	4	5
Examples and additional comments:					
How well did I give specific feedback and personalised recognition when earned by the player(s)?	1	2	3	4	5
Examples and additional comments:					
How well did I implement the use of player reviews/monitor the player's effort levels and allow for feedback during the session?	1	2	3	4	5
Examples and additional comments:					
How well did I set up chances for the players to offer ratings of their effort/performance individually or as a collective?	1	2	3	4	5
Examples and additional comments:					
How well did I set appropriate challenges/goals for the players and adjust them when needed (i.e. goal met, too hard/easy)?	1	2	3	4	5
Examples and additional comments:					
How well did I encourage persistence after mistakes?	1	2	3	4	5
Examples and additional comments:					
How well did I encourage the players to approach (and not avoid) new skills/tasks and then praise them for it?	1	2	3	4	5
Examples and additional comments:					
How well did I recognise and praise players when their effort and/or persistence led to an improvement?	1	2	3	4	5
Examples and additional comments:					
Overall Commitment Session Score:					/ 40

Communication Session Evaluation					
Answer the questions below circling the closest and most honest response. Then add any examples and comments to the question that you feel will help you improve in that area for your next session. The rating scale is as follows: **1** = Not at all; **2** = Infrequent/Poor; **3** = Moderately well; **4** = Quite well/Appropriately; **5** = Very well/At all appropriate times					
How well did I include and use strategies that highlighted the player's communication skills?	1	2	3	4	5
Examples and additional comments:					
How well did I recognise and praise players who demonstrated 'helping' and 'encouraging' skills?	1	2	3	4	5
Examples and additional comments:					
How well did I recognise and praise players when they 'praised' and 'acknowledged' their teammates?	1	2	3	4	5
Examples and additional comments:					
How good was I at identifying players who gave negative communication and teaching them appropriate alternative behaviours?	1	2	3	4	5
Examples and additional comments:					
How well did I recognise and praise players who demonstrated good listening skills, either to a teammate, or me as the coach?	1	2	3	4	5
Examples and additional comments:					
How much did I encourage players to share examples of a teammate's good communication that left the teammate feeling valued?	1	2	3	4	5
Examples and additional comments:					
How much did I encourage players to share examples of a teammate's poorer communication, explain the effect it had and offer ways to support better?	1	2	3	4	5
Examples and additional comments:					
How well did I use player reviews/monitor the players 'HELPA' levels, to maintain and elevate communication level as the session progressed?	1	2	3	4	5
Examples and additional comments:					
Overall Communication Session Score:					/ 40

Answer the questions below circling the closest and most honest response. Then add any examples and comments to the question that you feel will help you improve in that area for your next session. The rating scale is as follows: **1** = Not at all; **2** = Infrequent/Poor; **3** = Moderately well; **4** = Quite well/Appropriately; **5** = Very well/At all appropriate times

How well did I identify and explain the correct sensory cues that the players can practice focusing on during the exercises in the session?	1	2	3	4	5

Examples and additional comments:

How well did I use the strategies and exercises to highlight and improve the player's narrow-external (performing) focus, and in the midst of distractions?	1	2	3	4	5

Examples and additional comments:

How well did I use the strategies and exercises to highlight and improve the player's broad-internal (decision making) focus?	1	2	3	4	5

Examples and additional comments:

How well did I use the strategies and exercises to highlight and improve the player's narrow-internal (responding/preparing) focus?	1	2	3	4	5

Examples and additional comments:

How well did I use the strategies and exercises to highlight and improve the player's broad-external (scanning) focus, and in the midst of distractions?	1	2	3	4	5

Examples and additional comments:

How well did I recognise and praise when a player showed good concentration during the session, particularly under pressure/distractions etc?	1	2	3	4	5

Examples and additional comments:

How good was I at identifying when a player showed poor concentration and offering them ways to refocus?	1	2	3	4	5

Examples and additional comments:

How well did I implement the use of player reviews/monitor concentration levels and look to elevate it as the players began to tire/lose focus?	1	2	3	4	5

Examples and additional comments:

Overall Concentration Session Score: / 40

Control Session Evaluation

Answer the questions below circling the closest and most honest response. Then add any examples or comments to the question that you feel will help you improve in that area for your next session. The rating scale is as follows: **1** = Not at all; **2** = Infrequent/Poor; **3** = Moderately well; **4** = Quite well/Appropriately; **5** = Very well/At all appropriate times

Question	1	2	3	4	5
How well did I re-introduce and teach certain 'Rules of Engagement', and set up 'error management' rules that were reinforced throughout the session?	1	2	3	4	5
Examples and additional comments:					
How well did I include strategies that allowed the players to experience the benefits of positive emotional responses (e.g., relaxation zone; self-talk)?	1	2	3	4	5
Examples and additional comments:					
How well did I include strategies that allowed the players to experience the drawback of negative emotional responses?	1	2	3	4	5
Examples and additional comments:					
How well much did I encourage players to detach themselves from mistakes quickly (e.g. using "I'm Back!" as an error management rule)?	1	2	3	4	5
Examples and additional comments:					
How well did I recognise and praise when a player helped a teammate overcome a mistake/event (e.g. "Next Effort Tom!")	1	2	3	4	5
Examples and additional comments:					
How well did I recognise and praise a player who showed immediate alertness/positive and controlled responses to a mistake/event/break in play?	1	2	3	4	5
Examples and additional comments:					
How good was I at identifying when a player showed poor emotional control to a mistake/event/break in play and show them the appropriate behaviour?	1	2	3	4	5
Examples and additional comments:					
How well did I implement the use of player reviews/monitor the players' levels of control throughout the session, and challenge them to maintain/improve?	1	2	3	4	5
Examples and additional comments:					
Overall Control Session Score:					/ 40

Confidence Session Evaluation

Answer the questions below circling the closest and most honest response. Then add any examples or comments to the question that you feel will help you improve in that area for your next session. The rating scale is as follows: **1** = Not at all; **2** = Infrequent/Poor; **3** = Moderately well; **4** = Quite well/Appropriately; **5** = Very well/At all appropriate times

How well did I organise my session to increase in difficulty and allow for each player to achieve gradual accomplishments?	1	2	3	4	5
Examples and additional comments:					

How well did I encourage and set the tone for players to act 'confident' throughout the practice session and practice a resilient physical presence?	1	2	3	4	5
Examples and additional comments:					

How good was I at directing praise and specific feedback to individual players on their accomplishments and efforts?	1	2	3	4	5
Examples and additional comments:					

How well did I develop a 'no fear of failure' climate by encouraging players to persist and approach new challenges in conjunction with praise for intentions?	1	2	3	4	5
Examples and additional comments:					

How good was I at recognising and praising players who looked and performed confidently?	1	2	3	4	5
Examples and additional comments:					

How good was I at recognising and praising players who acknowledged and supported the confidence of a teammate?	1	2	3	4	5
Examples and additional comments:					

How much did I allow players the chance to focus and showcase their strengths by giving them the options of favourite and feel good drills?	1	2	3	4	5
Examples and additional comments:					

How well did I implement the use of player reviews and check in with players to help maintain and elevate positive attitudes throughout the session?	1	2	3	4	5
Examples and additional comments:					

Overall Confidence Session Score:	/ 40

5C Reflection Month: Coaching Evaluation

During your '5C reflection' months, use this evaluation sheet to help you identify where your players are currently in learning and demonstrating the behaviours and responses of the 5Cs. Use this review to help you plan ahead to specifically target those areas that are still in need of further work during the coming months.

What evidence was there in the session of the players 5Cs in action?

Commitment:

Communication:

Concentration:

Control:

Confidence:

What impact do you think the training session (and the individual practices) had on the players 5Cs?

Commitment:

Communication:

Concentration:

Control:

Confidence:

What do you believe were the most prominent behaviours and responses shown during the session?

What do you believe were the least prominent behaviours and responses shown during the session?

To what extent do you believe your choices of practices affected the behaviours and responses shown by the players? Give examples.

To what extent do you feel you own behaviour affected the 'Cs' shown by the players during the session? Give examples.

Based on your observations, what areas do you think need additional work on, both in terms of the player 5C use and your own behaviours and responses?

Players:

Coach:

Planning Ahead for Next Season

Fast forward a year. You've just finished your first season implementing the 5Cs coaching process with your players. How do you know how it went? How will you judge the success of your players' 5C skill development through the year? How do you know what to work on next season to keep progressing your players further? Being able to answer these and similarly intended questions is important in being able to successfully analyse the myriad of information available to you regarding performance, and apply it toward driving your players' 5C development further in future years.

When the time comes to formulate the next season's development plan it is useful to reflect on the objectives you set at the beginning of the previous season. Using the annual plan provided over the previous page we have set hierarchical objectives, whereby to achieve the seasonal aims requires achieving the cycle aims, which in turn requires achieving the individual 5C coaching phase objectives. Operating in this manner ensures a coherence to the annual plan and a clarity over what is trying to be achieved. So your first step is to simply take each objective in turn and answer the questions: "Have we achieved this objective?" and "What evidence is there to support that assertion?"

If you have followed our recommendations regarding evaluating your 'C' training sessions using the reviews sheets provided, you will have a vast library of information that will help you decide on how successful you have been at reaching your objectives. Other information that you may wish to tap into, to support your own personal reflections immediately after each session, might be the views and opinions of your players, observations made during matches, recorded footage of training and matches, and/or the view of the players' parents. This may be considered quite an onerous task to complete, however by considering as many different sources of information as possible, together they will add up towards a more complete picture of success, giving you more certainty moving forward with your planning.

After completing this diligent review you will have a pretty comprehensive list of competencies that your players were, and were not, successful in achieving. Those needing further work are obvious behaviours to carry forward and target next season. Depending on the level of review you conducted - the skills, behaviours and responses you have identified may be at the level of the team, unit, individual, or all three. The more individualised you can be with your analysis, the stronger and more effective your new annual plan will be.

With this information you can now begin to look for overarching themes which may inform your overall objectives for the season, cycles, and specific 'C' coaching phases. For example, across your squad it may have been a reoccurring theme during the control phase, and the reflection months, that not only were there a growing number of players who beat themselves up over mistakes in important matches, but that teammates failed to remove them from their mistakes. As a consequence your objectives for the coming season may focus on increasing your players' awareness of this problem. Specifically you may target work on improving their reactions to mistakes, and creating positive teammate support structures during the control coaching phase.

It is worth noting, however, that your planning doesn't need to solely focus on the players' weaknesses. You may wish to ease your players back into using their 5Cs by building in a 'recap' period for each 'C' at the beginning of a new phase. Alternatively you may wish to specify in the programme the times where you will address some of the weaknesses identified from the previous season. This may be part of each session, once a week, or a couple of sessions each phase. This will leave you with more time to focus your attention on more 'positive coaching' by building on the players' 5C strengths, or working on areas the players may highlight as ones they want to work on week-by-week.

Next it is important to consider any expectations or any cognitive, behavioural or social 'milestones' that may occur due to the development age of the player. These will need to be factored into your planning. For example, the potential inversion of effort and ability of an 11 year old, or the growing influence of peers. The information we have provided in each of the individual 'C' chapters should help you with this, along with your own personal experiences. These developmental milestones need to be identified and managed carefully, as they will heavily influence your planning and coaching of the related 'C'. Failing to plan for them does have the potential to derail and undermine even the best of plans.

Having reached this stage in your planning you should be in a position to attempt setting your team's objectives to guide your coaching throughout the coming season. As previously mentioned, the more specific the information you have recorded throughout the season, the better informed you will be when coming to plan for the next one. This will allow you to delve deeper into your planning beyond the wider team plan, to the specifics of an individual plan for each player. For example, your end of season review may have highlighted that one of your players has regularly struggled with his concentration in defensive situations at key times in training and matches. Therefore you decide that one of this player's seasonal objectives is to improve their ability to concentrate under pressure in defensive situations. This player's first cycle objective might be to improve their ability to focus at key moments during the game. Specific concentration phase objectives may be to train the player's 'mental effort' in order to develop the player's ability to focus and refocus when defending crosses and late on in matches. Though this process undoubtedly will require considerably more work on your part, it will allow you to cater each session for the individual needs of each player and ensure that each player's progression is not left to chance.

Finally when piecing your annual plan together it is important to keep it flexible. Whilst we would all love for our plans to move smoothly from one phase to the next, and for development occur at exactly the same rate as we planned, this is rarely the case (unfortunately). Some players will quickly take on-board and begin to demonstrate the behaviours, skills, and responses from each 'C', whilst others will need more time. More likely is that the same player will acquire some of the skills from one 'C' but find another 'C' more challenging. With this individuality it is important to plan to take advantage of the reflection months. These allow you built-in time to take stock, review the development of the players versus your plan, and then make the necessary adjustments for your second cycle and the rest of your season.

Closing Summary

Developing players' technical, tactical, and physical skills at any age is not something that many coaches are willing to leave to chance. Quite often meticulous planning goes into deciding which skills should be taught 'when' and in what order. Unfortunately it is our experience that this diligent planning is not often applied to the development of a young player's psychological and social skills. With the support of the example annual plan in this chapter, the hope is that you feel more comfortable in setting the direction for your players to work towards, and help them maximise their psychological skill development.

Using the 'C' review sheets regularly will serve to support the ongoing progression and development of the annual plan. They also serve as a reminder for you in term of how well you 'PROGRESS' each 'C' session-by-session. Such reflections on a week-to-week or month-to-month basis form a useful system for clubs in helping coaches to review the integration of psychology into their coaching curriculum.

9

Putting it all together: A 5Cs case study

In closing this 5C's guide for youth football coaches, we felt it important to present the reflections and insights from a professional youth academy coach who went through the first coach education project on the 5Cs. Intent on integrating psychological and social skills into youth academy football training, the academy coaches would receive an educational workshop from the first author (Harwood) focused on one of the 'Cs'. After each 90 minute workshop, coaches were asked to experiment with specific coaching behaviours and strategies related to that 'C' in their next four coaching sessions. After those four sessions the coaches received another workshop on the next 'C', and so the cycle continued until the final 'C' (confidence) had been practiced.

Over the following pages we provide you with a detailed account from one youth academy coach who went through this 'educate-practice-review' process across the season. In his account he details his experiences in integrating the 5Cs into his coaching practice.

The chapter is split into three main sections based on how we encouraged the coaches to view their sessions; namely a pre-training segment, the training session, and a post-training segment. The first section deals with the pre-training segment, or 'dressing room zone.' Here the coaches were encouraged to promote a particular 'C' and set it up for the forthcoming session, within the confines of the changing room. The second section progresses onto the pitch as the coach recounts how he offered opportunities for the players to develop and work on their 5C qualities. Finally in 'closing down' the session, the coach shares his experiences in how to conduct a post-session debrief in order to reinforce and consolidate learning.

Hopefully, presenting this true-to-life, practical insight will not only provide you with additional thoughts, but also strengthen your belief in the ideas you've already developed.

Targeting the value of pre-training preparation

"Before each training session we would always conduct a pre-session in the changing rooms with the players. We used this to develop the mindset of the boys prior to the session and it was important in helping to bring the group together and to allow the dynamics of the group to mix. These sessions lasted only 15 minutes as an average, but this was all dependent on developments in the session, such as how well discussion was going with the players. The benefit to having a session before going to train was that it allowed me to list the 5Cs objectives of the session with the team, small groups, or on an individual basis. The players would know the theme of the session we were going to focus on and also understand the expectations for the session.

Depending on the age group I was working with, we would only focus on one 'C' at a time. This was certainly true when I was working with the U9s and U10s, regardless of the time in the season. When I coached the U12s, once we'd been through each of the 5Cs I looked to add 'Cs' together to "load their minds". So after doing work on Commitment, I'd then do sessions that tied Commitment and Communication together."

Strategies to 'promote' and 'engage' the players in the 'C'

"It was important in these sessions that they were short, quick, so we could then move it to the training pitch. But at the same time they needed to be challenging, varied, interesting and fun. So I used a lot of different methods in order to introduce the 'Cs' such as using group work, discussions, DVDs, or match footage from the players themselves to analyse their own 5C actions. Imagination was the only real limit with this. This also gave me the opportunity to reinforce any themes I felt necessary from previous sessions, or from previous weeks.

We would use discussions a lot early on, asking lots open questions like "What do think we mean when we talk about your concentration?", "What is concentration to you?" or "Why is concentration important?" Other methods I used to help the players to understand a particular 'C' more was through using role models. If we were looking at passing during a training session, I'd ask the players who the best passer was in their opinion. Then to make him seem more real to the players I'd ask them to go away and find out as much information about that player as they could. When we did this with dribbling, the boys really got detailed with what they found out about Cristiano Ronaldo. In the end, as a group, we had Ronaldo's full name, where he played as a professional, someone found out which teams he played for when he was a teenager, how many brothers and sisters he had, where he grew up, his favourite colour, everything. They boys really felt they knew Ronaldo and related to him a lot more, which made the role model much more powerful when we referred to him in the training session because the boys felt they knew him.

Another tool I used during these sessions was caricatures. So, again using the example of dribbling, the players were in groups and between them they were given an outline of a footballer. They then had to draw only what a top dribbler needs onto the outlined player. We had one group draw big eyes onto the player because he needed to see, another drew dynamite on his legs because they felt a top dribbler needed to be explosive. We also had a playing card drawn on the leg of the player from a different group. When I asked why a playing card, the boy who drew it said it was because a top dribbler needs lots of tricks. They got really creative with it and I think it really helped them think about what traits a player needed for the different skills we used this for. I kept all these drawings and all the written work from these sessions and before the boys arrived for every session I'd stick them up on the walls of the changing room to reinforce the work we'd done."

Setting the right environment: Interactive, open and safe

"I often did as much as I could in terms of setting up the task. I'd explain learning points by writing and drawing diagrams on whiteboards. Particularly with the younger players I wanted to immerse them in the learning and cater for different learning styles. After this I would hand it over to the players to lead the direction of the session.

By handing it over I was trying to create a "team climate" during these sessions. It was necessary that after I set the task the players took over and the direction the session went after that was very much down to the players. They set the scene for the rest of the session. My job was then to move around each pair or group of players and listen to their ideas and solutions to the task they had been set. I would also make sure that when we were setting up a task, or feeding back as a group, that the players were organised in a semi-circle. This meant that no-one was stood in the background, or that no-one was more important or less important. Everyone was equal.

181

Another way I created a "team climate" was taking control initially over 'who worked with whom'. This was quite challenging to begin with. I didn't want the 'talkative' players to dominate the 'less talkative' players, so I made sure that every player would have a role in the exercises and that everyone worked with a different partner/group every session. An example of this was that we would have roles for players such as 'spokesperson' or a have a part of the session where a different player could go and 'steal' ideas from other groups and then feedback to his group what he found out. All of this was focused on developing an environment that was open, focused on relationships between players, and targeted their confidence in communicating and speaking their minds. In the end we ended up with a group of players who were positive communicators and this led to really great open discussions between the players and myself.

Because I wanted all the players to contribute equally, to become more confident and not be afraid in giving their opinion, we had a saying which I always started off the feedback section with. It was the 'the best thing to do is the right thing. The next best thing is the wrong thing. The worst thing to do is nothing at all.' I feel it was a nice little message that tied our commitment, communication and confidence ethos together. Both on and off the pitch we were sending the message that everyone should to be able to trust each other and feel comfortable with each other; standing up and giving a wrong answer was one step closer to getting things right, compared to hiding and not saying anything at all. We are all learning! Using this time before training helped me get that message across and help me grow the meaning of the message in the players"

A way to integrate new players

"The sessions before training were also a good time to start integrating any new players within the group. If we had a player joining us on trial, after introducing myself, I'd ask one of the boys to 'buddy-up' with the new player. His job was to help answer any questions the trialist had, as well as introduce him to the rest of the group. I'd explain that before the training session started they had to introduce themselves and before the end of the training session they had to find out something about the boy on trial and tell him something about them. During drinks breaks, I'd ask a boy what they'd found out about the trialist, as well as asking the trialist what he had found out about the rest of the players in the squad. Topics that the players found out from each other ranged from whether they had any brothers or sisters and what school they went to, to what club they'd played for and how many goals they'd scored in the previous season. All of this served the purpose of trying to integrate the trialist into the group, make him feel welcome and try and remove any nerves he had."

Using the Pre Session Time: A summary

This pre-training session became an important time in our integration of the 5Cs coaching programme. It allowed the coaches at each age group to begin engaging the players in the upcoming session. The coaches used this time to intentionally promote their chosen 'C' for the training session in a creative and interactive way. As you have hopefully seen, the important feature was that the players led the session, owned elements of it, or were heavily involved.

The coaches were encouraged to use this short time to develop a clear understanding of the 'C'-related behaviour and skills they wanted from the players during the session. The tasks helped the players to begin to understand the significance of the 'C' and to help clearly outline the outcomes of performing, or not performing, these targeted behaviours. The coaches would then give the players the opportunity to interact with each other in a non-threatening environment and facilitate a discussion around their feedback. In this way the players hopefully discovered for themselves why it is of benefit to them to possess these skills.

The coaches also used this time to work with their players to establish their expectations for the session, setting realistic goals for the players to achieve. In doing so the coaches were setting their stall out in terms of the values and qualities that mattered to them. They were giving mental skills the same level of importance as technical skills or tactics, because to the coach (and therefore the players) they all played an equal role in being able to meet the demands of the game.

The main session: Coaching the C in training

"When conducting my training sessions I always included the 'C' we were working on in every part of training. So we have the 'C' in the warm-up, the 'C' in the technical practice, the 'C' in the skill practice, the 'C' in the small-sided game and the 'C' in the cool-down. I only aimed at working on one 'C' at a time with the U9s and U10s. When I worked with the U12s, we'd start working one 'C' at a time at the beginning of the season but later multiple 'Cs' would be worked on. Sometimes this was intentional when I felt I could 'load on' another 'C', sometimes this was unintentional. I'd sometimes see someone demonstrating a 'C' really well and want to highlight it, or feel that I needed to emphasise a bad reaction from someone because it was happening a bit, and so I'd introduce that 'new' 'C' to the session for that player or that team to work on for the exercise, or rest of the session."

Building the 'C' around the drill: Monitors, player support, role models and scenarios

"My choices of drills were often, but not always, restricted to what was on the club's training syllabus. But within that syllabus the drills we chose were set up to bring out the 'C' we wanted to work on. The types of drills I chose were open and random to allow the 5Cs mental skills to develop.

I'd go about educating the 5Cs within the drill by highlighting how important the 'C' was for the session. For example, using both good and poor examples of that 'C' and putting it in the full context of the game. I would also use examples and role models from other sports. Role models in particular were so important to be able to show both good and bad examples. "Who showed good communication skills at the weekend? Are we showing those skills here?"

We'd also have the 'Cs' constantly promoted during the session by using player monitors. We'd select three or four players to essentially monitor how well they thought we were performing on our chosen 'C', and they would give a score out of 10. We chose three of four players so that we got varied opinions from the group. The players would have to justify why they felt we were a six in our communication and what they thought we needed to do in order to get a seven, for example. Then we'd agree from the monitors what score we were at and then the challenge for them was to improve on that score.

The drills I used also catered for both the players on the ball and off the ball. This was done by giving tasks to players off the ball such as observing other players and providing feedback to them and setting challenges for them to reach next time, or during a drill stopping the exercise and asking a player off the ball where their focus was and what cues they were looking for to help them decide what to do next.

This kind of player support happened more broadly as well during training sessions where players were encouraged to speak up and praise any player they felt did something well or spotted them doing any of the behaviours of the 'C' we were working on. This was important to me because they were all interacting and helping each other solve issues or problems and help each other improve each other's performance.

When I worked with the older age groups, the content and delivery of the training session would be more player-led. I also looked to see whether the players could use the 5Cs in more game-like situations, so the intensity of the sessions would be higher, with more decision making. The targets and expectations I had of the players would be more challenging, but realistic and achievable. For example, could they show positive behaviour and quick recovery after they had made a mistake, or could they show just as high a level of confidence to get on the ball and try new tricks to beat players when they were leading, compared to when they were losing?"

Developing the 'C' throughout the practice: Observation, modelling and personalised feedback

"The most challenging part of incorporating the 5Cs was making the decision of when to move on with the content and how fast - thereby trying to balance the needs of all individuals. In order to tackle this I introduced the idea of a 'clinic'. Basically this involved me taking out players to receive 'treatment' at the 'clinic'. So those players who were seen to be 'behind' could get extra support and helped to be successful at the drill. Then they would leave the 'clinic' and be put back into the drill and monitored. An example of this from one session I had was when we had a player who was very self-critical. I 'made an appointment for him at the clinic' and he came out of the drill for 'treatment'. There we had a little chat about calming him down and explaining how to bin mistakes during the drill. He then left the 'clinic' with the task of trying to do what we had talked about.

Players didn't always enter the 'clinic' for 'treatment'. Sometimes a player left the drill to speak to me to reassure that player and discuss what area the player felt they could improve on from within the drill. I then challenged them to improve that skill for the rest of drill. It was important to do this so that it wasn't just the 'weaker' players who kept coming out of the drill, as the players would spot that and it would make the whole 'clinic' a very negative thing. So the perceived 'better' players would also have to come out of the drill. The ethos of it was that everyone can improve and everyone should strive to get better at their own pace.

Another method I used with the U9s and U10s was essentially a guessing game. Either during the whole training session, or during a drill, I'd challenge a player (or group of players) to show the rest of the players the 'C' I had asked them to show. So if we'd been working on Commitment, I'd ask the player to try and show behaviours and skills linked to Communication. Before we'd start a drill I'd ask the rest of the players to try and pick out clues in order to guess which 'C' they thought this player (or group of players) were showing (i.e. Communication), whilst they worked on the 'C' we'd been working on previously (i.e. Commitment). At the end of the drill I'd get the players in and ask them which 'C' they thought it was and why.

If I was doing this throughout the entire training session I'd put four small different coloured squares down and assign a 'C' to each coloured square. Then after each drill I'd ask the players to go stand in the square of the 'C' they thought the other player(s) were showing. I'd do this after every drill so that the players could talk to each other in the down time about why one of them stood in the Control box and another stood in the Communication box. It also gave the players a chance to change their mind if they wanted. Sometimes if I picked several players to demonstrate a new 'C' to the players during a drill for the others to guess, I'd give them the same 'C' (i.e. I'd ask them all to show Concentration, whilst everyone else was working on Communication). This way when the players were trying to guess, we could also discuss what the differences and similarities were in how each player showed Concentration. Then we would introduce Concentration to the players."

Coach behaviour: Influencing the 'C' through communication and feedback

"Over the course of the session I'd say I attempted to behave in a relaxed manner so the players felt at ease in the learning environment. What I mean by that is not asking too much of the players so they feel under-pressure to achieve the goals of the drills, or feel afraid of being creative and practicing with their 5Cs in case it went wrong. To help, I always told the players that I was always learning alongside them during training sessions, that they might say something that I hadn't thought of, or that might be better, so I learn from them and together we get better. This often means that, as a coach, you need to listen and not just talk.

An example of what I mean by this is that in one training session I didn't think we were training as well as we had been. I brought the players in and asked if they understood what we were trying to achieve in the drill, which was about concentration, specifically scanning the field to help our movement off the ball. The players said they understood, so I asked if they felt I was being too harsh on them in expecting them to be performing better. One player put his hand up and said he felt that I was being too harsh. I asked him why he felt that and he backed down and changed his mind. I asked the player to be honest and said that if he did then I would set myself a goal of making sure I didn't ask too much of the group, and he had to set himself the goal of not backing down with his opinion. The boy agreed and said that he felt I was being too harsh on the group and he felt they just needed a little bit more time to get to grips with the task, because he felt they didn't quite understand.

After he had backed up his opinion I put a cone on the floor between myself and boys. I asked them to look at the cone. I said "when I look at the cone I can only see one side of it, whereas from where you are you see a completely different side. So sometimes I might have to come across to your side and look at the cone from your perspective to see what you see, just as you might have to come round to my side to see what I see. That way together we can agree how we can improve".

This incident was really important because it helped me keep an eye on my behaviours and expectations as the coach, to keep them in line with those of my players. For my players, it helped them feel more confident and braver in communicating their thoughts and thinking independently. Between myself and the player who voiced his opinion we had said to the group that we had an open environment for learning and that no-one should be afraid to speak up. As a result I had more and more players coming up to me and what improvements they could make. Together we had strengthened the communication, the commitment, and the confidence of the team.

When giving feedback to the group to review and reinforce as we go along, I think it is important not just to praise the player that has given you the answer. Quite often when I ask the players a question several hands go up. Once I've chosen a player to answer the question and he's given me the answer I'm looking for, the hands go down from everyone else. But the players who put their hands down when the right answer was said, also had the right answer. They just didn't get praise for it because I picked someone else to answer the question. So I think it is important not only to praise the player with the correct answer but also say "...and well done to you as well, because I could see you had the right answer too." That way when I ask the next question they will be just as enthusiastic and willing to answer it."

Making the down time 'live'

"Restarts to the session after drinks breaks were another opportunity to instil the 5Cs coaching points we had been working on. It was also a useful time to get the players to re-focus on the drill we were about to start. I'd do this by asking the players "Where did we leave the last drill?" and after some feedback from the players I'd ask them "Are we ready to build on that in the next drill?" This helped re-affirm the standards we'd agreed on before the session and learning that we had done to that point, as well as challenging the players to improve throughout the session."

Putting into practice: The transfer from training pitch to match day

"An example of how something we worked on in training could be seen working in matches was from our work on Control. We'd worked on different ways the players could overcome a mistake or an error during a game such as, imagining that as they return to their position they are 'entering a new room' that was better and that once they'd entered the room they had to 'close the door' behind them. In other words, closing the door on their mistake. Other ways we used were to pick up a blade of grass and throw it away and as they did that they had to imagine they were throwing away the mistake, challenging themselves and each other to move on past a mistake after they cross a white line on the pitch, or simply when they are ready and past the mistake show a thumbs up. In fact the 'thumbs up' was very popular with my U9s. During matches, whenever someone made a mistake there would be a pause and then the player would look to me and put his thumb up at me. At that point I knew he was fine and he was past the error and ready to go again.

Another example of putting practice into match day was during warm-ups where I used the idea of the 'silent versus vibrant' theme from the Communication training sessions. We'd start the warm-up in silence and gradually by introducing certain players with communication roles for example encouraging the players, we built up to a crescendo of noise by kick-off with everyone energised to play."

Conducting the main session: A summary

The main session is where the coach has the most opportunity to reinforce messages from the pre-session segment and create a consistent climate that values one or more of the 'Cs'. Using the P.R.O.G.R.E.S.S. acronym (see chapter 2), the coach has a series of golden opportunities to create and progress drills that challenge players to demonstrate and practice a 'C', whilst using modelling, reinforcement and praise to influence the thoughts, feelings and behaviour of players. This also includes creating responsibility in peers, as peer monitors or peer coaches, so that certain skills or actions are recognised and acknowledged by other members of the squad, not only the coach.

The art for every coach is being able to serve as a source of knowledge for players about mental skills, and to be innovative in creating exercises and conditions that help players to apply that knowledge and build competence through the use of reinforcement and problem solving.

'Closing down' the session: The value of post training reflection

"At the end of each session a discussion always took place between the players and myself. This may have been as a whole group discussion, or sometimes dividing the group into threes or fours before bringing them back as a whole group to feedback. Typically I'd ask the players to think about: how they felt the session went; what they thought they did well; what they thought they could improve on, and what they wanted to achieve in the next session. I'd always aim to really focus and highlight the positives and try to get the players leaving with a spring in their step, looking forwards to the next session. It was also important to have the players give a reason why they felt things went well, or didn't go so well.

The idea behind this was that it helped bring out what learning had taken place and how much the players had understood. This was good for me so I could plan adjustments to the content of future practices so that we weren't moving too quickly.

Another type of debrief that we used frequently was to speak to each player individually. As we were tidying up equipment, I'd call out each player and I'd ask them for one thing they did well at during the session, and one thing they would like to improve on during the next session. I'd then bring the whole group together to re-affirm some of the good things that I'd been told by the players and ask the players to think of a way they could work on the area they picked out for improvement away from training. It was important to always remind the players that top players spent extra time outside training sessions practicing their skills, such as David Beckham staying behind after training to practice his free kicks and crossing technique.

189

As a result of this we were keeping the players' motivation to train very high. We were constantly setting new goals for the players to achieve session-upon-session. This meant we also had to include a review of how well the players had done at making steps to work on the area they wished to improve on - as part of our debrief sessions.

Though I think it is important for the entire group to be together at dispersal, I always made myself available to the players so they could come and speak to me separately. Players who wished to clarify a task, who didn't quite understand something I said during the session, or who just wanted to talk generally about their performances, were more than welcome to do so. This was something that happened more so with the older age groups I coached.

With the younger age groups I coached I found myself making a few suitable changes to the way I did my debrief sessions. I found myself using a lot more diagrams and drawings to help the younger players understand more easily what we had gone through. The information and level of detail they were expected to go into was also much more diluted.

Typically this process would take us about 15 minutes to do. I know that can sound like a lot of time, especially at the end of a training session, but it was very important to me to do. I learnt a lot about what the players had and had not understood. It also meant I could make the players feel special and feel like they all had the same opportunity to improve. My role was simply to pose probing questions and then listen."

Using post session debriefs: A summary

Once the coach brought his final exercise to an end, it was important to 'close' the session down appropriately. This was a two-part process that asked the coach and players to collaboratively review and reinforce the quality of their 5C skill use during the session. Building in this form of self-reflection from an early age is an important part of developing good commitment and self-regulatory behaviour. It can also act as a process to set the direction for future training sessions and promote the skills and behaviours the group would be working on in the future. This provides players with a clear roadmap of where they are going with their development from one session to the next.

In reviewing the training session the coach acted as a facilitator to allow the players to self-reflect on their performance. This self-reflection by the players served to strengthen the learning that had taken place during the session and helped the players take more ownership over their own performance. Done in a positive and constructive manner, debriefing after a training session carries significant learning potential in order to help the team understand the application of the 5Cs for the benefit of their performance.

Having now read through our youth coach's account of how he integrated the 5Cs across his coaching, it may be useful for you to pause and reflect on how you now might integrate some of these examples within your coaching before, during, and after training. If you are joined by a group of coaches whilst reading this, it may be a useful exercise to do in a group, or separately before sharing and discussing your ideas. To help, you may wish to consider the following to stimulate debate:

- How might you promote your chosen 'C' in a creative, innovative, and enjoyable way for your age group?
- How might you role model and show value towards the 'C' of your choice?
- How might you manage the group so that everyone feels their contribution matters across all three sections of training?
- How might you create an open and positive learning environment across all three sections of training?
- In what ways might you involve the players in the learning process and progress behaviours within and over sessions for your age group?
- How will you know if the players have assimilated what they've learnt?
- How would you go about helping players feel confident enough to voice their opinions?

Reflecting on developing psychologically confident coaches

When starting out this theme of work as a sport psychologist, the first question I asked myself was *"What psychological coaching goes on when the coaches coach?"*. It was important to decipher what psychological outcomes might be experienced by players, or what psychological effects (i.e., on motivation, confidence, communication, concentration, and self-control) the coach is

191

having on a young player. In terms of increasing the confidence that coaches possessed for having a psychological impact on their players, they needed a user-friendly roadmap and framework that made sense. What immediately made sense to them was the issue of 'value' and identity - that basic psychological and interpersonal skills should be allocated the same importance and identity as tactical, technical and physical skills. Hence, they understood the purpose of 'role modelling' psychological skills or behaviour as a coach, and introducing the value of such a skill in different and creative ways whilst being in the presence of the players (as sponges of new knowledge). Using the 5C's framework, there are many ways beyond the training session that coaches can impact on the young footballer. The 5C's approach to matches and matchday is a completely different book and topic, yet inseparably tied to what coaches have developed as their training philosophy.

In conclusion, we believe that coaches play an important and critical role in assisting with the psychological development of youth footballers. For talented players to reach their full potential and cope with the challenges they may face in the modern game, they can usefully draw on all elements of the 5Cs. Some coaches may focus on the technical or physical competencies of the young player. However, neglecting a consistent focus on these mental skills and qualities can constrain a young player's development and coping abilities. Therefore the challenge for the modern coach is to integrate mental skills creatively by structuring the 5Cs seamlessly within their normal training sessions. By creating a positive and functional psychological climate in your coaching, you fulfil a coaching role that we believe will help to develop tougher, smarter and more confident performers who both embrace and enjoy the challenges of the game. This coaching legacy not only relates to the minority of youth players who gain the opportunity to achieve their professional dreams, but also the hundreds of thousands of players who become more psychologically and socially skilled through their experiences of your coaching.

10
Summary of coaching strategies and behaviours

As you will have noticed whilst reading through the practices for each 'C', many of the strategies we have proposed to help 'add in' and emphasise a 'C' can have multiple outcomes. For example, whilst you may select *Silent Soccer* as a strategy to increase your players' awareness of the importance of communication, or improve their use of non-verbal communication, this strategy can also be used to develop elements of your players' concentration skills. Therefore the purpose of this section is to bring together all the strategies we have used throughout the book and provide a summary that outlines which 'Cs' are influenced by that particular strategy.

To make this a quick and useful index that you can return to time and time again and to pinpoint the strategies you wish to use within your training practices, we have located the chapter and practice where the strategy is initially presented. The more confident that you become in coaching the 5Cs, the more you can use this index to help you pinpoint strategies in order to develop multiple 'Cs' within your coaching sessions.

Coaching Strategies and Behaviours Summary

Strategy	Location		Targeting the C's					Development Phase	
	Chapter	Practice	Commitment	Communication	Concentration	Control	Confidence	5-11	12-16
Adjusting the Challenge	Confidence	Trigger	●	•	•	•	•	•	•
Appraise Effort	Commitment	Pass and Move	●	•	•	•	•	•	•
Best Response Ever	Control	King of the Road	•	•	•	●	•	•	•
Better HELPA	Communication	Tag Game with Corner Boxes	•	●	•	•	•	•	•
Breathing, Body Language, Self-talk	Control	Pass and Move	•	•	•	●	•	•	•
Coach Confidence	Confidence	King of the Road	●	•	•	●	●	•	•
Commentator Football	Concentration	Support Play Possession Pratice	•	•	•	•	•	•	•
Communication Confidence Booster	Communication	Communication Focused Match	•	●	•	•	●	•	•
Communication Triggers	Communication	King of the Road	•	●	•	•	•	•	•
Concentration Triggers	Concentration	Switching Pitches Small Sided Game	•	●	•	•	•	•	•
Control Monitoring	Control	King of the Road	•	•	•	●	•	•	•
Copying Confidence	Confidence	Trigger	●	•	•	●	●	•	•
Emotional Confidence Booster	Control	Courage Under Fire	•	•	•	●	●	•	•
Emotional Oscar Winners	Control	Playing with Emotions Game	•	•	•	●	•	•	•

Location			Targeting the C's					Development Phase	
Strategy	Chapter	Practice	Commitment	Communication	Concentration	Control	Confidence	5-11	12-16
Extra Time	Concentration	Trigger Word Small Sided Game	●	●	●	●	●	●	●
Freeze Frame-Fast Forward	Concentration	Support Play Possession Practice	●	●	●	●	●	●	●
Future-Proof Coaching	Commitment	Breakout Game	●	●	●	●	●	●	●
Group Collaboration	Commitment	Pass and Move	●	●	●	●	●	●	●
Group Work	Communication	King of the Road	●	●	●	●	●	●	●
HELPA Check Up	Communication	Trigger	●	●	●	●	●	●	●
Individual Rules of Engagement	Control	Tag Game with Corner Boxes	●	●	●	●	●	●	●
Interference and Distractions	Concentration	King of the Road	●	●	●	●	●	●	●
Maintaining Focus	Concentration	King of the Road	●	●	●	●	●	●	●
Man-to-Man Marking	Concentration	Support Play Possession Practice	●	●	●	●	●	●	●
Most Controlled Player Award	Control	Playing with Emotions Game	●	●	●	●	●	●	●
Most Distracted Player Ever	Concentration	Accurate Passing	●	●	●	●	●	●	●
Opposed Practice	Communication	Pass and Move	●	●	●	●	●	●	●
Oscar Winning Communication	Communication	Trigger	●	●	●	●	●	●	●

Strategy	Chapter	Location Practice	Targeting the C's Commitment	Communication	Concentration	Control	Confidence	Development Phase 5-11	12-16
Oscar Winning Concentration	Concentration	Trigger	○	○	○	○	○	○	●
Peer Error Management	Control	Bad Refereeing Game	○	●	○	●	●	●	●
Peer "Yes!" Football	Confidence	Tag Game with Corner Boxes	○	●	○	○	●	●	●
Personalised Feedback	Commitment	Trigger	●	●	○	●	●	●	●
Positive Football	Control	Courage Under Fire	○	●	○	●	●	○	●
Relaxation and Readying Zone	Control	Pass and Move	○	○	○	●	○	○	●
Second Phases	Concentration	Trigger Word Small Sided Game	●	●	○	○	●	●	●
Setting a Goal	Commitment	King of the Road	●	●	○	●	●	○	●
Sharpen the Senses	Concentration	Pass and Move	○	●	○	●	●	○	●
Silent Soccer	Communication	Communication Focused Match	○	●	○	○	○	○	●
Silent vs. Vibrant Soccer	Communication	Communication Focused Match	○	●	○	○	○	○	●
Simon Says	Communication	Support Play	○	●	○	○	○	○	○
Stepping it Up	Confidence	Pass and Move	●	○	○	○	●	●	●
Sweat "o" Meter	Commitment	King of the Road	●	○	○	○	○	●	●

	Location			Targeting the C's					Development Phase	
Strategy	Chapter	Practice	Commitment	Communication	Concentration	Control	Confidence	5-11	12-16	
Switching Channels	Concentration	Tag Game with Corner Boxes	●	●	●	●	●	●	●	
Team Captain	Communication	Pass and Move	●	●	●	●	●	●	●	
Team Emotional Management Rules	Control	Bad Refereeing Game	●	●	●	●	●	●	●	
Team Work	Commitment	Breakout Game	●	●	●	●	●	●	●	
Toughness Tests	Control	Bad Refereeing Game	●	●		●	●	●	●	
"Yes!" Football	Confidence	King of the Road	●			●	●	●	●	
What is Control?	Control	Trigger		●	●	●	●	●	●	
Which Pitch?	Commitment	Trigger	●	●	●	●	●	●	●	
World's Worst Communication Ever	Communication	Defending as a Defensive Unit		●	●	●	●	●	●	
World's Worst Response Ever	Control	Playing with Emotions Game	●	●	●	●	●	●	●	

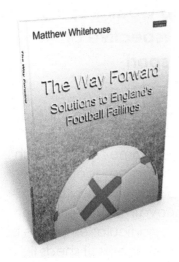

The Way Forward: Solutions to England's Football Failings

by Matthew Whitehouse

English football is in a state of crisis. It has been almost 50 years since England made the final of a major championship and the national sides, at all levels, continue to disappoint and underperform. Yet no-one appears to know how to improve the situation.

In his acclaimed book, The Way Forward, football coach Matthew Whitehouse examines the causes of English football's decline and offers a number of areas where change and improvement need to be implemented immediately. With a keen focus and passion for youth development and improved coaching he explains that no single fix can overcome current difficulties and that a multi-pronged strategy is needed. If we wish to improve the standards of players in England then we must address the issues in schools, the grassroots, and academies, as well as looking at the constraints of the Premier League and English FA.

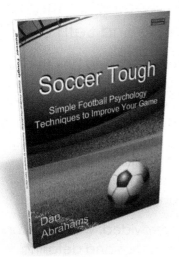

Soccer Tough: Simple Football Psychology Techniques to Improve Your Game by Dan Abrahams

"Take a minute to slip into the mind of one of the world's greatest soccer players and imagine a stadium around you. Picture a performance under the lights and mentally play the perfect game."

Technique, speed and tactical execution are crucial components of winning soccer, but it is mental toughness that marks out the very best players – the ability to play when pressure is highest, the opposition is strongest, and fear is greatest. Top players and coaches understand the importance of sport psychology in soccer but how do you actually train your mind to become the best player you can be?

Soccer Tough demystifies this crucial side of the game and offers practical techniques that will enable soccer players of all abilities to actively develop focus, energy, and confidence. Soccer Tough will help banish the fear, mistakes, and mental limits that holds players back.

Scientific Approaches to Goalkeeping in Football: A practical perspective on the most unique position in sport
by Andy Elleray

Do you coach goalkeepers and want to help them realise their fullest potential? Are you a goalkeeper looking to reach the top of your game? Then search no further and dive into this dedicated goalkeeping resource. Written by goalkeeping guru Andy Elleray this book offers a fresh and innovative approach to goalkeeping in football. With a particular emphasis on the development of young goalkeepers, it sheds light on training, player development, match performances, and player analysis. Utilising his own experiences Andy shows the reader various approaches, systems and exercises that will enable goalkeepers to train effectively and appropriately to bring out the very best in them.

Developing the Modern Footballer through Futsal by Michael Skubala and Seth Burkett

Aimed at coaches of all levels and ages, Developing the Modern Footballer through Futsal is a concise and practical book that provides an easy-to-understand and comprehensive guide to the ways in which futsal can be used as a development tool for football. From defending and attacking to transitional play and goalkeeping, this book provides something for everyone and aims to get you up-and-running fast.

Over 50 detailed sessions are provided, with each one related to specific football scenarios and detailing how performance in these scenarios can be improved through futsal. From gegenpressing to innovative creative play under pressure, this book outlines how futsal can be used to develop a wide range of football-specific skills, giving your players the edge.

The Modern Soccer Coach: Position-Specific Training by Gary Curneen

Aimed at football coaches of all levels, and players of all ages and abilities, The Modern Soccer Coach: Position-Specific Training seeks to identify, develop, and enhance the skills and functions of the modern soccer player whatever their position and role on the pitch.

This book offers unique insight into how to develop an elite program that can both improve players and win games. Filled with practical no-nonsense explanations, focused player drills, and more than 40 illustrated soccer templates, this book will help you – the modern coach - to create a coaching environment that will take your players to the next level.

The Footballer's Journey: real-world advice on becoming and remaining a professional footballer by Dean Caslake and Guy Branston

Many youngsters dream of becoming a professional footballer. But football is a highly competitive world where only a handful will succeed. Many aspiring soccer players don't know exactly what to expect, or what is required, to make the transition from the amateur world to the 'bright lights' in front of thousands of fans. The Footballer's Journey maps out the footballer's path with candid insight and no-nonsense advice. It examines the reality of becoming a footballer including the odds of 'making it', how academies really work, the importance of attitude and mindset, and even the value of having a backup plan if things don't quite work out.

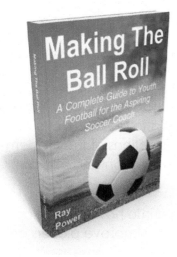

Making The Ball Roll: A Complete Guide to Youth Football for the Aspiring Soccer Coach by Ray Power

Making the Ball Roll is the ultimate complete guide to coaching youth soccer.

This focused and easy-to-understand book details training practices and tactics, and goes on to show you how to help young players achieve peak performance through tactical preparation, communication, psychology, and age-specific considerations. Each chapter covers, in detail, a separate aspect of coaching to give you, the football coach, a broad understanding of youth soccer development. Each topic is brought to life by the stories of real coaches working with real players. Never before has such a comprehensive guide to coaching soccer been found in the one place. If you are a new coach, or just trying to improve your work with players - and looking to invest in your future - this is a must-read book!

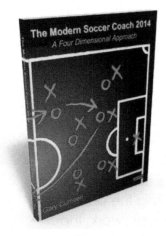

The Modern Soccer Coach by Gary Curneen

Aimed at Soccer coaches of all levels and with players of all ages and abilities The Modern Soccer Coach 2014 identifies the areas that must be targeted by coaches who want to maximize a team's potential – the Technical, Tactical, Physical, and Mental sides to the game. See how the game has changed and what areas determine success in the game today. Learn what sets coaches like Mourinho, Klopp, Rodgers, and Guardiola apart from the rest. Philosophies and training methods from the most forward thinking coaches in the game today are presented, along with guidelines on creating a modern environment for readers' teams. This book is not about old school methodologies – it is about creating a culture of excellence that gets the very best from players. Contains more than 30 illustrated exercises that focus on tactical, technical, mental, and physical elements of the game.

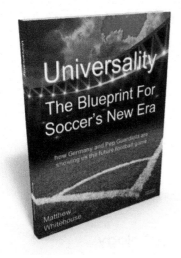

Universality | The Blueprint for Soccer's New Era: How Germany and Pep Guardiola are showing us the Future Football Game by Matthew Whitehouse

The game of soccer is constantly in flux; new ideas, philosophies and tactics mould the present and shape the future.

In this book, Matthew Whitehouse – acclaimed author of The Way Forward: Solutions to England's Football Failings - looks in-depth at the past decade of the game, taking the reader on a journey into football's evolution. Examining the key changes that have occurred since the turn of the century, right up to the present, the book looks at the evolution of tactics, coaching, and position-specific play. They have led us to this moment: to the rise of universality.

Universality | The Blueprint For Soccer's New Era is a voyage into football, as well as a lesson for coaches, players and fans who seek to know and anticipate where the game of the future is heading.

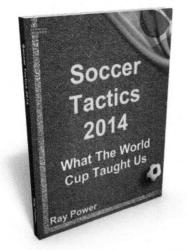

Soccer Tactics 2014: What The World Cup Taught Us by Ray Power

World Cups throw up unique tactical variations. Countries and football cultures from around the globe converge, in one place, to battle it out for world soccer supremacy. The 2014 World Cup in Brazil was no different, arguably throwing up tactical differences like never seen at a competition in modern times.

Contests are not just won by strong work ethics and technical brilliance, but by tactical discipline, fluidity, effective strategies, and (even) unique national traits. Soccer Tactics 2014 analyses the intricacies of modern international systems, through the lens of matches in Brazil. Covering formations, game plans, key playing positions, and individuals who bring football tactics to life - the book offers analysis and insights for soccer coaches, football players, and fans the world over. Whether it is Tiki-Taka, counter-attacking, or David defending heroically to defeat Goliath - this book sheds light on where football tactics currently stand… and where they are going. Includes analysis of group matches, the knock out stages, and the final.

Other Recent Books from Bennion Kearny

What Business Can Learn From Sport Psychology
by Dr Martin Turner & Dr Jamie Barker

The 7 Master Moves of Success
by Jag Shoker

**Paul Webb Academy: Strength Training Books
for Footballers and Goalkeepers**

Learn More about our Books at:

www.BennionKearny.com/Soccer

Lightning Source UK Ltd.
Milton Keynes UK
UKOW07f2231061216
289103UK00038B/456/P